# Modern
## Cake Decorating

# Modern
# Cake Decorating

by
AUDREY ELLIS

**HAMLYN**
LONDON · NEW YORK · SYDNEY · TORONTO

© Copyright this edition 1976
The Hamlyn Publishing Group Limited
London · New York · Sydney · Toronto
Astronaut House, Feltham, Middlesex, England

ISBN 0 600 36209 4

*First published by George Newnes Limited 1965*
*Third impression 1968*
*Revised edition 1976*
*Fifth impression 1978*

Printed and bound in Spain
by Graficromo, S. A. – Córdoba

# Contents

# USEFUL FACTS AND FIGURES

## NOTES ON METRICATION

The Hamlyn Group has worked out a plan for converting Imperial measures to their approximate metric equivalents. Exact conversion from Imperial to metric measures does not give convenient working quantities, so for greater convenience the metric measures have been rounded off into units of 25 grams. The following table shows the amounts to the nearest whole figure and the recommended equivalents.

| Ounces/fluid ounces | Approx. g. and ml. to nearest whole figure | Recommended conversion to nearest unit of 25 |
|---|---|---|
| 1 | 28 | 25 |
| 2 | 57 | 50 |
| 3 | 85 | 75 |
| 4 | 113 | 100 |
| 5 (¼ pint) | 142 | 150 |
| 6 | 170 | 175 |
| 7 | 198 | 200 |
| 8 | 226 | 225 |
| 9 | 255 | 250 |
| 10 (½ pint) | 283 | 275 |
| 16 (1 lb.) | 456 | 450 |
| 20 (1 pint) | 569 | 575 |

As a general guide, 1 kg. (1000 g.) equals 2.2 lb. or about 2 lb. 3 oz.; 1 litre (1000 ml.) equals 1.76 pints or about 1¾ pints. This method of conversion gives satisfactory results in nearly all recipes; however, in certain cake recipes a more accurate conversion may be necessary to produce a balanced recipe.

**Liquid measures** The millilitre is a very small unit of measurement, so for ease it is recommended that decilitres (units of 100 ml.) are used. In most cases it is perfectly satisfactory to round off the exact millilitre conversion to the nearest decilitre; thus ¼ pint (142 ml.) is 1½ dl.; ½ pint (283 ml.) is 3 dl.; ¾ pint (428 ml.) is 4 dl. and 1 pint (569 ml.) is 6 dl., or a generous ½ litre. For quantities over 1 pint, use litres and fractions of a litre following the conversion rate of 1¾ pints to 1 litre.

## OVEN TEMPERATURE CHART

| | Fahrenheit | Celsius | Gas Mark |
|---|---|---|---|
| Very cool | 225 | 110 | ¼ |
| | 250 | 120 | ½ |
| Cool | 275 | 140 | 1 |
| | 300 | 150 | 2 |
| Moderate | 325 | 160 | 3 |
| | 350 | 180 | 4 |
| Moderately hot | 375 | 190 | 5 |
| | 400 | 200 | 6 |
| Hot | 425 | 220 | 7 |
| | 450 | 230 | 8 |
| Very hot | 475 | 240 | 9 |

As different makes of cooker vary and if you are in any doubt about the setting it is recommended that you refer to the manufacturer's temperature chart.

Glucose syrup (liquid glucose) is obtainable from a chemist.

## NOTES FOR AMERICAN USERS

| Imperial | American |
|---|---|
| 1 lb. butter | 2 cups |
| 1 lb. flour | 4 cups |
| 1 lb. granulated or castor sugar | 2 cups |
| 1 lb. icing or confectioner's sugar | 3½ cups |
| 1 lb. brown sugar | 2 cups (firmly packed) |
| 8 oz. stoned dates | 1¼ cups |
| 1 lb. dried fruit | 3 cups |
| 4 oz. chopped nuts | 1 cup |
| 8 oz. glacé cherries | 1 cup |
| 4 oz. cocoa powder | 1 cup |
| **Liquid measures** | |
| ¼ pint liquid (milk, stock, water, etc.) | ⅔ cup |
| ½ pint liquid | 1¼ cups |
| 1 pint liquid | 2½ cups |

The Imperial pint is 20 fluid ounces whereas the American pint is 16 fluid ounces.

The following list gives American equivalents or substitutes for some terms, equipment and ingredients used in this book.

| Imperial | American |
|---|---|
| Baking tin | Baking pan |
| Bicarbonate of soda | Baking soda |
| Cake mixture | Batter |
| Cocktail stick | Wooden toothpick |
| Cocoa powder | Unsweetened cocoa |
| Cornflour | Cornstarch |
| Deep cake tin | Spring form pan |
| Desiccated coconut | Shredded coconut |
| Double cream | Whipping/heavy cream |
| Greaseproof paper | Wax paper |
| Glacé cherries | Candied cherries |
| Icing bag | Pastry bag |
| Icing tube | Nozzle/tip |
| Patty tins | Muffin pans/cups |
| Single cream | Coffee cream/half-and-half |
| Sultanas | Seedless white raisins |
| Vanilla essence | Vanilla extract |
| Vanilla pod | Vanilla bean |

# Introduction

IF you enjoy making cakes, you already know how satisfying it is to put a cake on the table that not only tastes delicious, but looks really attractive. Looks influence taste so much, it is not surprising that your cakes will receive many more compliments if they are beautifully decorated.

Cake decorating is undoubtedly a most rewarding art but, like any other, requires study and practice in the techniques which produce the happiest result—a harmonious design carried out with craftsmanship which is not necessarily difficult to learn.

Perhaps you have tried your hand at this art, and been rather disappointed with the finished cake, or perhaps you are a complete beginner? Whether you are a cook of some experience or have never yet iced a cake, you will find in this book all the help you need to make a success of the job. With its aid you will soon solve all the little mysteries of this fascinating craft, including a full explanation of those tiresome technical terms you may have encountered in other books and found puzzling.

Do read the first five chapters carefully before you attempt to carry out any of the many designs given later in the book. You may be surprised how simple are the professional cake decorator's "tricks of the trade". However, it is essential to know them, and to practise the work of preparing the cake, planning a design and carrying it out, just as a professional would, to get the same perfect finish. Your decorations may never achieve this geometrical precision, but they will certainly do you credit and win you praise.

In any case, the designs given in such detail here are only a basis for your own experiments and the exercise of your own creative ability. That is the joy of decorating cakes. If you like simple patterns, many of these are included and, like most simple but good ideas, are extremely effective. For the woman who really enjoys the artistic self-expression of creating and carrying out ambitious designs of her own, and has time for this delightful hobby, there are many happy hours ahead with the aid of this book.

Audrey Ellis

# Decorating Equipment

MUCH of the equipment used for decorating cakes is already to be found in most kitchens. It is useful to have a special shelf where you can keep together all the small items that might easily be lost (icing syringes and tubes, paint brushes and tweezers, and so on). But provided they are quite clean and dry when you start work, there is no need to keep a special set of larger items such as basins and measuring jugs.

I have arranged the list of equipment required in two sections. First, items you probably have in your kitchen or elsewhere in the home, or can easily make. Second, those you will more probably have to buy.

Later in this chapter and throughout the book you will find explained more fully how all these things are used.

SECTION 1: Several glass or china basins of various sizes from $\frac{1}{2}$ to $1\frac{1}{2}$ pints capacity. Several wooden spoons of various sizes. A table knife. A spatula. A fine nylon sieve. A palette knife. Several table forks and teaspoons. A fine skewer or large pin for marking designs. A pair of scissors. String for measuring circumference of cakes. A pastry brush. Several small water-colour paint brushes. A pair of tweezers. Waxed and greaseproof paper. A hand rotary beater, whisk, or electric mixer. A packet of wooden cocktail sticks to use as picks. A pick board for drying off sugar flowers. A piece of thick cardboard with a 2-inch deep slit in one side to facilitate removing flowers from picks. A permanent template made of plywood (unless you intend using a Cake Marker or greaseproof paper templates) for marking designs.

SECTION 2: Icing syringes or icing bags of several sizes. An icing screw (which is needed to fit tubes to some icing bags). A selection of tubes. Rimless tubes to fit greaseproof paper icing bags. Meringue tubes (large) for piping meringue and fresh whipped cream. A turntable. A plain icing scraper for smoothing sides of cakes. A serrated icing scraper for making patterns. A set of flower nails. Net nails of various shapes. A long metal ruler or plastic Cake Decorator's Rule for smoothing tops of cakes. A Cake Marker.

Of course you will not need all these items until you attempt really elaborate piped decorations, and your stock of equipment can be added to and improved over the years.

**Basins:** It is a good plan to use small basins for preparing small amounts of icing. If a relatively large area is exposed to the air it will dry out and form a crust quickly. Metal basins are less suitable for icing than china or glass because they tend to become stained by certain food colourings or by acetic acid.

**Spoons:** A spoon with a large bowl is most useful because it beats up the mixture more quickly. When not being used it should not be left in the basin but scraped down and removed, the surface of the icing being covered with a damped piece of greaseproof paper or a damp cloth placed over the bowl. Be especially careful that wooden spoons are clean—grease may impregnate the wood.

**Knives:** A palette knife is useful, but do not choose one that is too flexible, as it must not bend too readily when you are using it to smooth firm icing. For scraping out icing basins, a spatula is more efficient.

**Sieves:** Fine-meshed nylon sieves are ideal and should be kept exclusively for dry goods such as flour and sugar. Do not use your sugar sieve for liquid. It is always worth

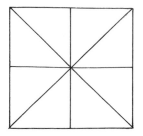 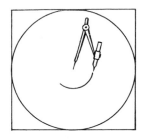 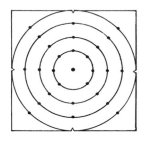 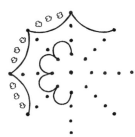

while to sieve icing sugar several times to make sure that it is smooth.

The kind of pencil-and-compass set used by school children can be used by the cake decorator; so can children's good quality paint brushes. Brushes that shed hairs, however, will mar your delicate tinting operations. Blunt-ended eyebrow tweezers are obtainable from most chemists, and are better than pointed ones which are inclined to dent sugar decorations as you lift them into place.

Greaseproof paper is invaluable for many purposes, especially for making icing bags when you are using small quantities of several different coloured icings. It is better to pipe out separate sugar flowers and other separately made decorations on waxed paper, as they will be easier to remove.

To make the wooden picks on which sugar flowers are piped, trim one pointed end off a wooden cocktail stick with a sharp knife, leaving the stick about 2 inches long. The blunt end passes through a hole in the pick board and rests on the table top. Children's games sometimes include a pick board for scoring, but if you have to make one, by far the easiest method is to cut a piece of pegboard about 8 × 12 inches, and nail two 1-inch wooden battens down the short sides,

or support it during use on two books of even thickness, placed under opposite ends.

You will also find it useful to have a piece of thick cardboard about 6 × 8 inches, with a 2-inch slit, about ¼-inch wide, cut in one of the long sides. To remove sugar flowers from picks, you slide the pick along the slit, and remove the pick downwards, leaving the sugar flower resting on the cardboard, where you can easily slip it off onto a sheet of greaseproof paper.

**How to make a permanent template:** (See the diagrams above.) You will need an 8-inch square of plywood and a small drill. Mark off centres of all four sides. Draw lines connecting the four corners diagonally and the centres of the opposite sides. This will give you the central point of the template and by placing the compass on this point and drawing round a circle of 4-inch radius, you will find you have a circle and square divided into eight parts. Draw in concentric circles of 1-inch, 1¾-inch, 2½-inch and 3¼-inch radius round the same point. Mark dots along the dividers beginning at the outer edge, at every point where these are crossed by the circles, which should leave a clear circle of 1-inch radius round the central dot. Drill fine holes through all these dots.

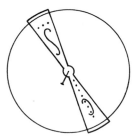 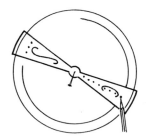 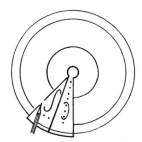 

The template can be placed over any round or square cake (on large cakes adjust so that the cake projects evenly on all sides) and a series of guide marks can be pricked out through it with a pin to make evenly spaced loop, garland or triangular designs. Plain round cutters and boat-shaped patty tins can be used as guides for the actual shape of semi-circles and ellipses after the template has been removed.

**How to use a Cake Marker:** (See diagrams below left.) The "Tala" Cake Marker is an alternative to the template, made from two

distances from the cake edge. The pivot is now exactly at the centre of the cake, and has to be fixed in position with a pin. To mark concentric circles insert pin or pencil in a hole of the wedge and swivel it round the centre until the circle is completed. To make wedge-shaped sections use one part of the marker or the two wedges hinged together and mark close to the sides of the wedge. Most patterns combine both methods of marking and when the important points have been marked the rest of the design can be pricked in with a pin or very fine skewer.

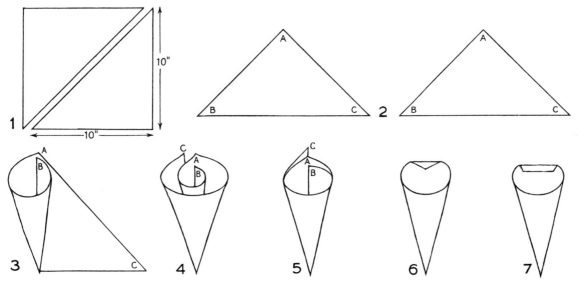

wedge-shaped pieces of plastic which are hinged together. Their common pivot is pierced so that the marker can be fixed into position with a pin. One of the wedges is pierced at equal distances with holes large enough for pin or pencil to be put through. One wedge is equal to $\frac{1}{16}$ of a circle but the two wedges can be hinged together to form $\frac{1}{8}$, $\frac{1}{10}$ or $\frac{1}{12}$ of a circle, and cake tops can be divided up accordingly. First find the centre of the cake. Open the marker so that the centre lines of the two wedges form one straight line across. Place on cake top and move about until the wedge ends are at equal

**How to make an Icing Bag:** Cut a 10-inch square of greaseproof paper across diagonally to form two triangles. Each one will make a separate bag. Take one at a time. Until you are practised in making icing bags, mark the three corners A, B and C as shown here to help you follow the directions for folding. Take corner B and fold it so it comes inside point A. Bring corner C round the outside of the bag so that it lies exactly behind A. See that all the three corners are together and the point of the bag is quite closed. Fold point A over twice to keep the bag together. Snip a small piece off the point for line piping, or cut off a larger piece of the bag and drop in a tube for fancy work. Do not cut off more than absolutely necessary to allow the fancy end of the tube to protrude, or pressure will cause the tube gradually to force out through the end of the bag. The bag should be about half filled with icing. The top can then be folded over about $\frac{1}{2}$ an inch, and folded over again several times until close to the contents. The two "tips" caused by this folding can then be brought in to the centre, and the right thumb pressed down on this join to force out the icing, directing the bag with the other four fingers spread loosely out round the outer curve. The left hand may be used to support the inner curve but this should not be absolutely necessary.

Cut the end off the bag at an acute angle to pipe leaves and flowers without a tube.

Don't be tempted to make the bag larger so that it holds more icing, as this makes piping difficult. The larger bag will need far more strength exerted from the wrist to press out the icing, which will tire the wrist and make your hand unsteady. If used too long, the bag will tend to split from the heat and moisture of the hand. Before beginning work, make up a number of bags. Those not used can be placed one inside the other stored in a larger polythene bag ready for another occasion.

**Material Icing Bags:** You may prefer to use a bag made of washable material, which is stronger and will hold more icing, for large jobs. These are available in sealed surface nylon and cotton, Porosan, linen and rubberised material suitable for butter icings. The standard sizes are $9\frac{1}{2}$, 12 and 15 inches. Nylon and Porosan bags can take an ordinary tube (with screw top) dropped into them and worked well down into the end. Other bags are intended to be fitted with a brass or plastic screw which fits the thread of the tube. Turn the bag inside out, tie in

the screw with a piece of strong thread, turn right side out again, and screw in the tube you wish to use.

**Metal Syringes:** Many housewives feel more at ease using a metal syringe than any other form of icing implement, because it can be firmly gripped and is easy to handle. Here, the flow of icing is controlled by a plunger, with a resilient plastic washer which slides down the barrel of the syringe and prevents the icing from rising above it. The plunger passes through the lid of the syringe which fastens with a bayonet catch. The icing then cannot escape except through the tube which is screwed to the other end of the syringe, under the pressure of the plunger.

**Filling:** Care is needed to fill the metal syringe to avoid air locks in the icing. Spoon it in with the first tube you intend to use ready by you. Make sure the icing fills the syringe evenly to about $1\frac{1}{2}$ inches from the top. Insert the washer, tilted at an angle, at the side of the syringe and swing over into the upright position making sure the washer fits exactly into the barrel. Press down the lid and lock into position with a slight clockwise turn. Continue pressing until icing appears, then screw in the tube at once. The right thumb fits naturally into the ring at the top of the plunger, the first and second fingers through the loops at either side of it. The barrel is lightly supported by the left hand.

To fill other icing bags, put the prepared bag with tube already inserted in the end, into an empty jam jar. This will hold the bag upright for filling. Fold back at least one third of the length of the bag to avoid getting the edge sticky with icing, and drop in the icing, which will usually fill the bag by its own weight. Lift and shake slightly if the icing does not fill in evenly. Now twist the bag firmly just above the level of the icing and hold firmly in the twisted position with

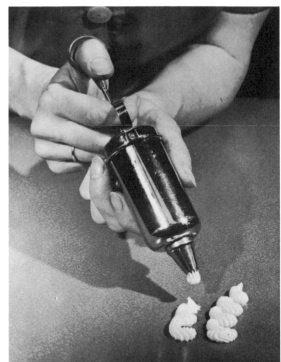

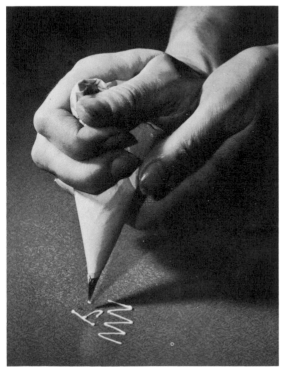

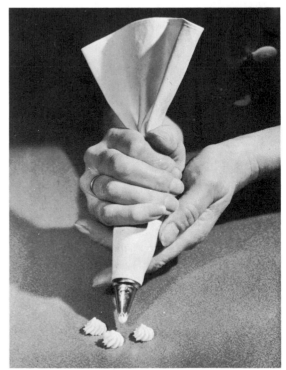

13

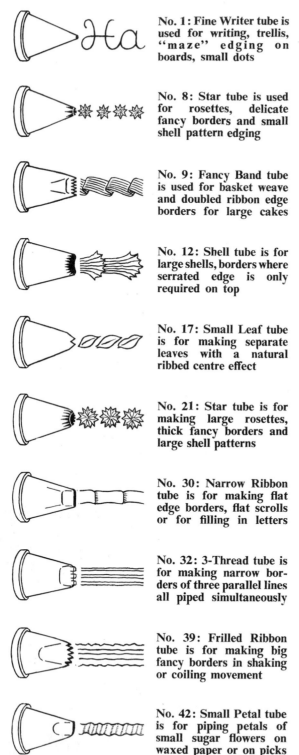

**No. 1:** Fine Writer tube is used for writing, trellis, "maze" edging on boards, small dots

**No. 8:** Star tube is used for rosettes, delicate fancy borders and small shell pattern edging

**No. 9:** Fancy Band tube is used for basket weave and doubled ribbon edge borders for large cakes

**No. 12:** Shell tube is for large shells, borders where serrated edge is only required on top

**No. 17:** Small Leaf tube is for making separate leaves with a natural ribbed centre effect

**No. 21:** Star tube is for making large rosettes, thick fancy borders and large shell patterns

**No. 30:** Narrow Ribbon tube is for making flat edge borders, flat scrolls or for filling in letters

**No. 32:** 3-Thread tube is for making narrow borders of three parallel lines all piped simultaneously

**No. 39:** Frilled Ribbon tube is for making big fancy borders in shaking or coiling movement

**No. 42:** Small Petal tube is for piping petals of small sugar flowers on waxed paper or on picks

the right (guiding) hand, supporting the weight of the bag if necessary in the palm of the left hand. When refilling with icing, replace in the jam jar, turn back the top and put in more icing. Scrape down the inside of the bag with a spatula as some of the icing will have worked up towards the top under pressure. Twist the bag again, making sure no icing is above this part of the bag. With care, piping need not be a messy job, and it will take much less time in the end if you spend a few more moments preparing the icing bag cleanly. If the icing is stiff enough for piping it will not run straight through the tube under its own weight. If this happens, the icing mixture is too thin to hold a shape when piped, and requires more sugar.

**Tubes, or Nozzles:** There are plastic tubes available which are very easy to keep clean, but for sharpness of outline, I prefer to use metal tubes. Examine tubes carefully when you buy them to make sure that they are perfectly finished inside and the design clearly cut. There are 42 standard patterns of screw-thread tubes, a further range of rimless tubes for use with paper icing bags, but the numbers quoted in this book are for the former, not the latter. When choosing these it is better to do so by general description such as "large star", "small petal", or "small leaf" tube, to avoid confusion over the numbers. The tubes illustrated on this page are among those most commonly used, and in fact few of the cake designs in this book require more than three different tubes.

**Cleaning:** Never use a metal skewer or other pointed object to clear tubes or they will become broken or misshapen. Soaking in very hot water will always clear them. Wash all tubes and material icing bags, and metal parts or syringes in very hot water, plastic washers in warm water. Dry thoroughly after cleaning. Metal parts can be dried off in a warm oven, bags by inverting over a milk bottle or jam jar in a warm place.

# Basic Icing Recipes

THERE are a great many different types of icing, cooked and uncooked, shiny or dull, hard or comparatively soft, but all have one thing in common. The basic ingredient is sugar. Of these, royal icing is the most frequently used for elaborately decorated cakes.

## ROYAL ICING

Sieve the icing sugar twice. To each pound of icing sugar, allow at least two large egg whites. (In many cases three will not be found too much, but eggs vary considerably in their weight and size, and also in proportion of white to yolk in their contents.) Separate the eggs carefully, taking care no trace of yolk gets into the white. Leave overnight in the refrigerator if possible to toughen the whites and make a firmer icing. Put the whites into a grease-free large mixing bowl, break up with a fork, and add half the sieved sugar together with 1 teaspoonful strained lemon juice or 3 drops of acetic acid (which may be obtained from the chemist). Increase the amount of lemon juice or acetic acid in proportion of another teaspoonful lemon juice for every pound of sugar.

Whisk *slowly and steadily* until the mixture becomes very white and begins to stiffen. This will take at least five minutes. Beating the mixture too fast aerates it too much and makes it appear stiffer than it really is. For the second stage, gradually beat in by hand with a wooden spoon as much more icing sugar as is required to produce the correct consistency. The icing should form soft peaks for a coating consistency, but should be considerably stiffer for piping work. For this reason it is better to make up a large quantity, use as much as is required for coating, and add more icing sugar to bring the rest up to piping consistency.

*Never use icing sugar without sieving it at least once, and preferably twice.* Storage conditions may have affected it adversely and could cause it to cake unless thoroughly sieved just before use.

When the icing is made, cover with a damp cloth and leave for at least an hour before using, to allow the air bubbles to subside.

British Sugar Corporation

15

Opinions differ on the merits of adding glycerine to royal icing. If the cake is to be used soon, lemon juice or acetic acid will harden the icing quickly. If it is to be kept some time after decorating before eating, the addition of glycerine will keep the icing from becoming unduly hard. If the cake is made in tiers for a wedding, the addition of glycerine may cause the upper tiers to sink somewhat into the icing of the lower tiers. But I personally find the icing is improved by the addition of $\frac{1}{2}$ teaspoonful glycerine to every pound of icing sugar and have not experienced this difficulty.

Many recipes for royal icing exist, giving various proportions of sugar, egg white, and lemon juice (or suggesting white vinegar or acetic acid instead of lemon juice) and the addition of a few drops of blue food colouring (or washing blue) to improve the colour, as royal icing has a tendency to develop a creamy look, rather than remaining a brilliant white. Experience will determine the one you find most satisfactory.

**Using an Electric Mixer:** Put the egg whites in a bowl, beat lightly with a fork. Add the icing sugar gradually on speed 1 or 2, then beat at speed 2 or 3 for at least 5 minutes but not more than 6 minutes. Allow to stand several hours or overnight if possible in a basin covered with a damp cloth before use.

Royal icing can be stored in airtight containers, such as Tupperware or screw-top preserving jars, for several days in the refrigerator. Never leave it exposed to the air so that it forms a crust.

**How to use left-over royal icing:** Since royal icing is rather expensive to make and it is hard to judge just how much you will need, it is useful to know how to use up a small quantity. Delicious peppermint creams can be made by adding two drops of peppermint essence and two drops of green vegetable colouring to a small amount of icing (or more

according to taste), and sufficient extra icing sugar to give a consistency firm enough to roll out on a board sprinkled with icing sugar. Roll out $\frac{1}{4}$-inch thick. Cut into shapes with small cutters, place on greaseproof paper to dry out.

**Pastilage Decorations:** These cake trimmings can be made and stored in an airtight tin, for weeks if necessary, before use. You will need to buy some gum tragacanth powder from the chemist, and add $\frac{1}{4}$ level teaspoon powder to each $\frac{1}{2}$ lb. royal icing. Sprinkle a board with icing sugar, place the icing on the board, sprinkle on the powder and knead it in together with sufficient additional icing sugar to give a pliable dough. As it dries out quickly, place an inverted basin over part of the dough while you mould the rest. Roll it out to $\frac{1}{4}$-inch thickness on a board lightly sprinkled with cornflour. Sprinkle more cornflour on top of the icing and pass the finger tips lightly over the surface until it becomes glossy. Cut out into fancy shapes with tiny cutters (stars, crescents, hearts and so on). Arrange on greaseproof paper to dry out thoroughly. If liked, when dry dip some of the shapes into melted chocolate to coat one half, or decorate with dots of melted chocolate, using a fine skewer.

## FLAT ICING
Sieve the icing sugar twice. To every $1\frac{1}{4}$ lb. of icing sugar allow two large egg whites. Bind the icing sugar to a stiff paste with the unbeaten egg whites. Knead on a board dusted with icing sugar until quite smooth. At this stage you can knead in food colouring, a few drops at a time, to tint the flat icing any pastel shade you wish. To use for covering cakes, divide icing in half, knead one half into a smooth ball and roll into a circle to fit the top of the cake exactly. Roll into position. Divide the remainder and roll each ball into a strip to fit half way round the sides of the cake. Seal well. (The icing

Roederer Rich Champagne

**Sweethearts Wedding Cake:** this romantic design with a delicate decoration
of pink hearts on the sides calls for a Champagne toast to bride and groom

Plate 1

McDougalls Cookery Service

**Silver Bells Wedding Cake:** simple and charming design which even a beginner can ice without difficulty—only three tubes are needed for the piping

Plate 2

may be handled much like almond paste.)

Here is another icing which is particularly enjoyed by children, because it has a distinct chocolate flavour, and yet can be made in pretty pastel colours. The secret lies in using special chocolate bars.

## MILKY BAR ICING

*3 Nestlé's Milky Bars; 1¼ lb. icing sugar; 6 table-spoonfuls water; colouring if required.*

Melt the Milky Bars together with the water in a basin, standing over a saucepan of hot water. Gradually stir in the sieved icing sugar and then add the colouring. At this stage, part can be transferred to another warmed basin, and the two batches tinted different colours. The icing is now of coating consistency, and the quantity given allows ⅔ of the mixture to coat the sides of a 7- or 8-inch sandwich cake, and for piping. The rest can be stiffened and rolled out like almond paste, to make a circle to fit the top of the cake, and a reasonable number of decorations. Add 6-8 oz. more icing sugar to the remaining ⅓, and extra colouring, or this batch of icing will be paler in colour. (More or less icing sugar can be used to vary the consistency for coating, moulding, or piping.)

## FUDGE ICING

*½ lb. icing sugar; 1½ oz. butter or margarine; 3 dessertspoonfuls milk; 1 tablespoonful golden syrup; flavouring and colouring.*

Put the fat, milk and syrup together in a strong saucepan, and heat until the fat is melted, *but do not allow to boil.* (If you have a sugar thermometer, heat to 150° F.) Remove from heat, allow to cool for a few minutes, and pour over the icing sugar. Beat well until smooth. Cool slightly, beating occasionally, until icing is thick enough to leave a good trail, then pour over the cake.

**Chocolate Flavour:** Increase milk by 1 dessertspoonful and blend with 1 rounded tablespoonful sieved cocoa.

**Coffee Flavour:** Replace 1 dessertspoonful milk with 1 dessertspoonful coffee essence (or same amount of powdered instant coffee dissolved in 2 teaspoonfuls hot water and cooled).

**Dragged Designs:** Fudge Icing lends itself particularly well to what are called dragged designs, which are achieved by marking the icing before it sets, first in one pattern, then another, "dragging" the pattern already marked on the icing to give very pretty effects. (An example will be found in the Tropical Banana Gâteau on p. 113.) Here are just two ideas, but with a little experiment you can produce many more of your own designs.

**Birds in Flight:** Using the tip of a round bladed knife, mark a continuous zig-zag line from one side of the top of the cake to the other, carrying each loop right out to the edge and keeping the loops close together (you will get about four in each direction on top of an 8-inch cake). Now draw the point of the knife across the loops in parallel lines at right angles, about 2 inches apart, always starting at the same side of the cake.

**Flower Face:** Using a 4-tined table fork, begin at centre of cake and mark a continuous spiral set of grooves, right out to the edge of the cake and finishing with a set of grooves right round the edge of the top of cake drawing off to nothing where the circle joins. Now working from the edge to the centre, draw eight evenly spaced straight lines with the point of a table knife, all joining at the central point.
NOTE: Do not start at the centre and work outwards. The petal effect is made by dragging the lines inwards.

17

The most commonly used icing for smaller cakes and gâteaux is certainly glacé icing. This type of icing is also the easiest to make, and in fact can consist of a simple mixture of sieved icing sugar and warm water.

As glacé icing tends to "lift" crumbs, it should not be used to coat a cut surface, and should be spread with a knife as little as possible, being allowed to spread from the centre over the top and sides by its own weight, merely being "helped" to run evenly with a knife. Remember also that in other countries this type is called Warm Icing, and the golden rule for success is to add only cold or lukewarm water to the sugar, and never to allow the icing to be heated above lukewarm temperature.

Glacé icing should be used at a fairly thick coating consistency, that is, when checked over the back of a spoon it should coat it thickly before running off.

## BASIC GLACÉ ICING

*8 oz. icing sugar; 2 tablespoonfuls water; squeeze of lemon juice if crisp surface is required; flavouring and colouring.*

Sieve the icing sugar into a basin which fits neatly into the top of a saucepan, filled with hot water to come half-way up the sides of the basin. Add warm water, and lemon juice if used, to the icing sugar, beat well for one minute. Add flavouring and colouring if desired, place basin over hot water and continue beating over low heat until the sugar has dissolved. At no time allow the icing to become more than lukewarm, or the surface will dry dull and tend to crack.
NOTE: Omit lemon juice for coffee and chocolate flavoured glacé icings.

**Orange or Lemon Flavour:** Substitute warm strained orange juice or orange squash for the water; or substitute 1 tablespoonful strained lemon juice for one tablespoonful water. A few drops of food colouring may

also be added to either of these icings and will much improve the appearance.

**Chocolate Flavour:** Put 2 oz. plain chocolate, broken up, into the basin with 1 tablespoonful milk and 1 tablespoonful water. Melt over the hot water. Add 4 oz. sieved icing sugar and beat well. If icing is too thick, add a few drops more warm water; if too thin, more sieved icing sugar.

**Coffee Flavour:** Substitute 1 tablespoonful coffee essence for 1 tablespoonful water.

## FEATHER ICING

Some really spectacular effects can be achieved with glacé icings of contrasting colours by "feathering". Originally this was done with the tip of a thin feather quill, but you will find a fine skewer most effective. The basic idea is to coat your cake with plain white icing, pipe lines with a fine writing tube or simple paper icing bag in a contrasting icing (pink or chocolate) on white icing while it is still wet, and then mark with the skewer to obtain a dragged effect. Alternatively, the basic icing may be chocolate and the feathering done in white or pale pink. A classic example of simple feathering is shown in the Mille Feuilles Gâteau on p. 94, and a most unusual way of feathering in the Iced Butterfly Cake on p. 88 (both of which also appear in colour plates). Here is another popular design, the Spider's Web.

**Spider's Web Design:** Mix 10 oz. sieved icing sugar to a stiff glacé icing, using very little warm water. Blend three teaspoonfuls drinking chocolate with enough boiling water to moisten it. Place one tablespoonful of the white icing into a small bowl, and add the blended drinking chocolate to it. Put into a paper icing bag. (This may be done without an icing tube. Do not cut off the end at this stage.) Spread the white icing over the top of the cake. Snip about $\frac{1}{8}$-inch off the end of

the piping bag, and at once pipe circles of chocolate icing on top of the white. Immediately, while still wet, using a skewer, draw eight evenly spaced lines out from the centre. Repeat from the outer edge in between these lines with another eight lines towards the centre, to give the web effect.

To fill rich cakes and for piped decorations butter creams and cream icings are often used, sometimes combined with glacé icing. The best combination is to fill the layers of the cake with a butter cream, reserve some of the remainder if wished for piping, and use the rest to coat the sides, which can be rolled in chopped nuts, chocolate vermicelli or sieved stale cake crumbs. The top of the cake is then easily covered with glacé icing and when this is dry, piped with butter cream.

## BASIC BUTTER CREAM

*4 oz. butter; 6-8 oz. icing sugar; flavouring and colouring if desired.*

Put the butter into a basin, beat until soft and creamy, add the sieved icing sugar a little at a time, beating well after each addition. The full amount of sugar may be added if a stiff icing is required to coat a cake, less if the butter cream is to be used as a filling. At this stage flavouring and

Cadbury Typhoo Food Advisory Service

19

colouring may be added. With rich chocolate and coffee cakes, the addition of a few drops of vanilla essence is all that is necessary as the colour makes a pleasant natural contrast.

**Coffee Flavour:** Add 2 teaspoonfuls coffee essence, a few drops at a time, to the icing before adding the last few tablespoonfuls of sugar.

**Chocolate Flavour:** Blend 1 tablespoonful cocoa with a little boiling water. Cool, beat in sufficient of this mixture to the butter cream to flavour as much as required.

**Peppermint Flavour:** Add a few drops each of peppermint essence and green food colouring to taste. Use for chocolate cakes.

**Orange Flavour:** Add the finely grated rind of half an orange and 1 tablespoonful strained orange juice or orange squash.

**Lemon Flavour:** Add the finely grated rind of half a lemon and 1 tablespoonful strained lemon juice or lemon squash, or 1 table-spoonful lemon curd and an extra ounce of icing sugar.

A less rich type of this icing can be made with either butter or margarine and the addition of milk. It is usually called Butter Icing, or Cream Icing.

McDougalls Cookery Service

## BASIC CREAM ICING

*3 oz. butter or margarine; 8 oz. icing sugar; 3 dessertspoonfuls milk; colouring and flavouring if desired.*

Put the butter or margarine into a basin, beat until soft and creamy, add half the sieved icing sugar. Beat well. Add the milk together with any desired colouring and flavouring, and then the rest of the sugar. Beat again until light and creamy. (In cold weather the milk may be warmed to blood heat.)

**Coffee Flavour:** Replace 1 dessertspoonful milk by 1 dessertspoonful coffee essence.

**Chocolate Flavour:** Replace 1 dessertspoonful milk with cocoa mixture as for Basic Butter Cream.

**Peppermint Flavour:** Add a few drops each of peppermint essence and green food colouring.

**Orange Flavour:** Add the finely grated rind of an orange and a few drops orange food colouring.

**Lemon Flavour:** Add 1 tablespoonful lemon curd and a few drops lemon food colouring. (Fruit juices are not advised to be added to this type of icing as they tend to make it curdle.)

Many variations can be achieved with simple sandwich cakes, filled with jam or lemon curd, and topped with Butter Cream or Cream Icing. The icing can be marked in many delightful patterns, and needs no further decoration; so it is quite easy to decide after lunch to make a decorated sandwich cake, bake it, cool it (preparing the icing while it cools), ice and decorate it, and have it ready for tea.

## PLASTIC ICING

4 *dessertspoonfuls water;* 4 *teaspoonfuls gelatine;* 4 *teaspoonfuls glycerine;* 4 *oz. liquid glucose;* 2 *lb. sieved icing sugar.*

Put the water and gelatine in a pan. Stir over a gentle heat until the gelatine has dissolved completely. Remove from the heat and add the glycerine and liquid glucose; pour into a bowl. Gradually add the icing sugar and mix to form a stiff paste. Sprinkle a working surface with cornflour and knead the paste until smooth.

This icing can be used in place of royal icing, to cover a rich fruit cake, and for moulding decorations. Any icing which is not being used must always be kept covered (under an upturned bowl, in a polythene bag or in a polythene container with a snap-on lid) to prevent it from hardening.

Brown & Polson Limited (Mazola Corn Oil)

**Flower Garland Cake: covered with plastic icing**

## FLOWER GARLAND CAKE

(Illustrated in colour on the jacket)

*Make up Rich Fruit Cake (using corn oil), see p. 127, in an 8-inch round tin.*

Make up 1½ lb. almond paste and use to cover the cake in the usual way. Make up 2 lb. plastic icing (see recipe opposite). Colour five-eighths of the icing with a few drops of yellow food colouring, kneading it in until the icing is an even colour throughout. Keep the icing covered until required.

Brush the almond paste-covered cake with egg white. Roll out the primrose-coloured icing on a board sprinkled with cornflour to approximately 12 inches in diameter. Place over the top of the cake and work the icing down the sides of the cake with fingers dipped in cornflour.

Shape the remaining white icing into about 60 daisies as follows, adding a little more icing sugar to make a workable paste (do not have it too stiff, otherwise the petals will have cracked edges): take a small piece of the icing and shape to form a small barrel. Using the rounded end of a pen (dipped in cornflour) make an indentation in one end, then remove the shape from the pen and snip with scissors to form six petals. Pinch with fingers to neaten petals. Allow to become hard and then colour the centres yellow, either with a dot of royal icing or plastic icing. (If preferred, yellow daisies may be made with white centres.)

Place the daisies on the cake in a decorative design as shown in the picture opposite, and intersperse with sprigs of fern. With royal icing, using a No. 12 shell tube, pipe a shell border around the bottom edge of the cake. Arrange daisies at regular intervals, with a sprig of fern coming from each daisy, to cover the edge of the board or plate.

An excellent and economical icing can be made using a solution of gelatine instead of white of egg. It is a smooth icing which coats better than glacé icing, and can be piped. It can be stored overnight in an air-tight container like royal icing, but should then be slightly warmed before using. Do not bring above blood heat, or it may crystallise.

## GELATINE ICING

*1 lb. icing sugar; 1 level teaspoonful powdered gelatine; food colouring if required.*

Dissolve the gelatine in ¼ pt. hot water and allow to cool. Sieve the icing sugar into a basin and add about 2 tablespoonfuls of the gelatine solution to it together with a few drops of any food colouring desired, and beat until it forms a thick icing similar to royal icing. Spread at once over the cake. This icing sets very much more quickly than royal icing. For larger quantities, allow that 1 tablespoonful of the gelatine solution equals one medium-sized egg white. Either make up another small batch when ready to pipe the decorations or store the remainder of the coating batch, and reheat just enough to soften to piping consistency when required.

## SATIN ICING PASTE

*1 oz. Table Margarine; 2 tablespoonfuls lemon juice; about 12 oz. icing sugar (12 well-heaped tablespoonfuls); food colouring if required.*

Melt the Table Margarine with the lemon juice in a medium-sized saucepan over a low heat (do not allow it to become hotter than blood heat). Add a few drops of food colouring if used. Stir in 4 oz. sieved icing sugar. Return to a very low heat until sugar has dissolved and mixture begins to bubble at the sides of the pan. Then continue to cook for 2 *minutes only.* Time mixture very carefully at this stage. If overboiled the icing may crystallise. Remove from heat and gradually stir in remaining icing sugar. Beat well with a wooden spoon until slightly cooled. Knead well on a board, using more icing sugar to make a smooth, pliable mixture. The longer the mixture is kneaded, the whiter it becomes. If the Satin Icing Paste is not to be used immediately wrap it in greaseproof paper and store in an air-tight tin, or place in a polythene bag and store in a cool, dry place. In this case, the icing should be kneaded again before using.

Fondant icing can be used either as an alternative to almond paste beneath a coat of royal icing, or as a finishing coat, but it cannot be piped.

## FONDANT ICING

Sieve the icing sugar twice. To each pound of sugar allow 1 egg white and 2 fluid oz. liquid glucose (obtainable from the chemist). Sieve the icing sugar into a large basin, make a well in the centre and add the egg white and glucose. Also add at least 1 teaspoonful almond essence, or any other flavouring preferred, and beat the mixture steadily, incorporating all the icing sugar into it gradually. Turn onto a board dusted with icing sugar, knead in a few drops of food colouring if required, and continue kneading until smooth and pliable. The method of coating the cake is rather like applying almond paste, as the fondant can be rolled out if kept dusted with icing sugar, but instead of cutting a piece to fit the top and strips for the sides, a large circle is applied to the top of the cake (which should first be brushed with egg white) and moulded down the sides. Any surplus is trimmed away at the lower edge.

NOTE: All icings are most susceptible to the atmosphere of the room in which you work. For instance, if it is very warm and dry they will tend to form a crust when left uncovered quite quickly, and to set quickly. In a cold, damp atmosphere, allow longer for setting.

# Preparing and Covering Cakes

As in most other expert jobs, a really professional-looking finish can only be achieved by spending time on the preparing and covering of the basic cake, especially in the case of iced and decorated fruit cakes. If this is done carefully you will get a perfect round or square top as the case may be, and straight sides. The icing will be perfectly smooth, and if you prick out the design to be piped through a template, the decorations will be really symmetrical, and you will be proud of the finished cake. Never try to fill in or disguise faults in the shape with icing. The time to do this is when you coat with almond paste or fondant, trimming the cake itself to even up, or building up gaps with small pieces of almond paste.

Here is the basic cake for the Stork Christening Cake (see p. 66) being prepared for decorating.

**Stage 1:** The cake, which in this case is perfectly shaped and needs no trimming, is brushed with a glaze, made from apricot jam brought to the boil and then sieved. If liked, a little water may be added to the jam before heating. A reasonable amount for a large cake can be made with ½ lb. jam and 2 tablespoonfuls water. Use a pastry brush to brush on the glaze thinly, and wash and dry the brush very thoroughly after use. If the cake has risen in the centre, trim flat, invert the cake and use base as top. In this case, fill in the sides round the base if needed with a long thin roll of almond paste, pressing it in firmly. Brush the cavity first with apricot glaze.

**Stage 2:** Divide the prepared almond paste in two. Roll one half of paste into a circle as nearly as possible the size of the top of the cake. Cut out, using cake tin as guide. Lift by half-rolling round the pin, and drop into place. Don't press down hard until the circle is right in position, then roll across lightly but firmly to seal to the top of the cake. Now roll remaining half of paste into a strip deep enough to cover sides of cake,

Stork Cookery Service

Stork Cookery Service

scraper all round to smooth. Allow to dry. You may decide to apply a second coat of icing, either because it is slightly uneven or is not thick enough. Follow the same procedure. Be sure to keep the basin of icing closely covered when not in use. Finish by taking a thin coating of icing out to the edge of the board. You may like to give a final third coat of thin glacé icing to obtain a very smooth shiny surface, but I find myself that two coats of royal icing are sufficient.

NOTE: The initial coating of almond paste or fondant is essential, to protect the icing from cake crumbs and from the grease and moisture of a rich fruit cake drying out and working through the icing.

allowing for trimming. Measure circumference of cake with string, trim strip of paste to fit exactly, and roll up like a bandage, having first lightly dusted it with icing sugar so that it will not stick to itself. (You may find it easier to handle if the length is divided into two, but this will mean making two seals instead of one). Unroll the strip of paste round the side of the cake, keeping the upper edge level with the top of the almond paste covering, taking care not to stretch the paste, and make the seal as neat as possible. Roll a clean empty jam jar round the sides of the cake to seal and smooth the strip in place. The cake is now ready for icing, but should be stored, covered, in a dry place for several days (a minimum of 2 days, a maximum of 7) before icing. If iced too soon, the almond oil from the paste may work through the icing and stain it.

**Stage 3:** Have the cake ready in position centred on a silver cake board, and anchor with a dab of icing. Spread icing over the top of cake first with a palette knife, which may be dipped in hot water, but must then be shaken quite dry before applying to the icing. Smooth with a metal ruler or cake decorator's rule. Allow top coat to dry. Spread icing round sides, then run an icing

**To coat a square cake with almond paste:** It is almost impossible to transfer a square piece of almond paste to the top of a large cake without spoiling the shape, so follow this method. Divide the paste into two portions. Roll out one piece into a square approximately the right size. Brush top of cake with apricot glaze and turn over on the square of almond paste. Trim away surplus with sharp pointed knife. Turn cake right side up again. Measure length and depth of one side and cut a strip of greaseproof paper to act as a pattern. Roll out remaining almond paste and cut four strips from the pattern. Brush sides of cake with apricot glaze and cover with strips of paste, one at a time. Join corners neatly, by pressing two rulers together to form a right angle against the paste.

## BASIC ALMOND PASTE

*6 oz. ground almonds; 6 oz. icing sugar; 6 oz. castor sugar; 1 standard egg; ½ teaspoonful each vanilla and almond essence.*

Sieve icing sugar into a basin and mix with the ground almonds. Put castor sugar and egg into another basin and whisk over a pan of simmering water until egg mixture is a little over blood heat. Remove from heat and whisk in the flavourings. Discard whisk. Stir in almonds and icing sugar and mix to a paste. Turn onto table generously dusted with sieved icing sugar and knead lightly until smooth and firm. Wrap in a polythene bag until required. (These quantities make just over 1 lb. almond paste.)

## RICH ALMOND PASTE

*12 oz. ground almonds; 6 oz. icing sugar; 6 oz. castor sugar; 1 teaspoonful lemon juice; ¼ teaspoonful almond essence; 1 large egg.*

Mix the ground almonds and sugars together in a basin. Stir in the lemon juice, almond essence, and the well-beaten egg. Turn out onto a board dusted with icing sugar. Knead lightly until smooth.

## ECONOMICAL ALMOND PASTE

*3 oz. fine semolina; 9 oz. ground almonds; 1½ lb. icing sugar; 1 egg beaten with 1 yolk; 3 dessertspoonfuls lemon juice; few drops each vanilla and almond essence.*

Mix together the semolina, almonds and sugar. Form into a paste with the remaining ingredients and knead till smooth and pliable.

## ALMOND PASTE (EGGLESS)

*12 oz. ground almonds; 4 oz. castor sugar; 4 oz. icing sugar; 5 level tablespoonfuls Nestlé's Condensed Milk; few drops each vanilla and almond essence; 1 teaspoonful lemon juice.*

Sieve together the ground almonds and sugars. Add the flavourings, condensed milk and other ingredients. Mix thoroughly with a wooden spoon, then press together with the hands into a ball and knead well. Roll out and use as required.

Shown right are two stages of another beautiful cake in the process of being covered, ready for piping, the Star-Time Christmas Cake (see p. 54). These photographs demonstrate different ways of smoothing the top and sides. First, the top with a long metal ruler which has been dipped in hot water and shaken dry, then the sides with a palette knife, held upright against the side of the cake with the right hand as the left hand slowly spins the turn-table. Be sure you hold the ends of the ruler well clear of the edges of the cake as you draw it gently across the top towards you with perfectly even pressure, or the top will not be flat, and you may damage the sides.

The ruler may force some icing over the sides, and you may have to repeat the processes of smoothing top and sides alternately two or three times before a clean edge is achieved.

Cadbury Typhoo Food Advisory Service

Above, the Star-time Christmas Cake is ready to mark out for piping. The feature of the decoration is the star shape in the centre, and here you see one method of marking out a design which does not lend itself to the sectional method (cake top divided into four, then into eight, etc.) because the star has an uneven number of points. A paper pattern of the star can easily be made to the exact measurements given, centred on the cake top so that all points are the same distance from the edge, and the shape pricked out round the pattern.

**Storing Fruit Cakes while decorating:** After coating with almond paste, allow from two days to a week before icing, but if time does not permit, make up a solution of 1 level teaspoonful gelatine powder to $\frac{1}{4}$ pt. hot water, and brush over the almond paste with this to seal. Allow to dry overnight and ice the next day. Allow plenty of time for each coat of icing to dry before applying another, or the second coat will tend to "lift" the first. Never try to put a stiffer coat of icing over a thinner coat. The outer coat or coats should be slightly thinner in consistency. In between the stages of icing, keep the cake covered from dust, either by sliding the cake

on its silver board into a large plastic bag that will not touch the icing, or by inverting a cardboard carton of suitable size over it.

If each stage of icing has dried out thoroughly before the next stage is carried out, there is little danger of the icing cracking and sinking under the weight of pillars used for wedding cakes. This trouble is often caused by applying more icing on top of a layer which has not quite dried out, sealing in the moisture which is trapped under an apparently hard surface which will not bear any weight. When the cake is finished it is safer to assemble the tiers and put the top decoration in place to make sure the position is correct, then dismantle the cake and store in its separate tiers until required. Do not attempt to transport it at all in the assembled state, or set it up long before required. Make sure the table is level and, if a trestle table, that the legs are firm.

**How to make a paper template:** When you wish to create your own design, experiment with a paper template. Using the cake tin as a guide, cut out a square. For round cakes, trim the template to a circle, or leave the four corners to assist you in moving it about. Measure the depth of the sides and the circumference of the cake with string after it has been iced, and cut a strip of greaseproof paper the same length plus $\frac{1}{2}$-inch overlap, and exactly the same depth. Now you are ready to create your pattern. As an example, here is a complete cake recipe and design for decorating.

## RASPBERRY LAYER CAKE
(Colour Plate No. 13)

*Make up Whisked Sponge Mixture No. 1 (see p. 124) in 2 7-inch sandwich tins.*

Split each cake into two layers, put together with alternate fillings of plain butter cream and raspberry jam. Make up 1 lb. Gelatine Icing (see p. 22) colouring it pink with a few drops of cochineal. Reserve about

⅓ of this for piping, and pour the rest at once over the top of the cake, smoothing round the sides with a palette knife. When icing is set, remove onto a silver cake board. Cut a 7-inch square of greaseproof paper, draw in a circle, divide into eight sections as for a permanent template. Using a tulip wine-glass as a pattern, draw semi-circles in each section. Fix to centre of cake with a pin. Now draw in a line ½ an inch from end of strip with pencil and ruler, for overlap. Place against side of cake so top of line joins one sectional divider on top of cake and mark point where next divider joins strip. Check measurement of circumference with this distance multiplied by eight, which should equal length of strip. Mark off strip into eight equal sections and fold into eight sections so that creases come at marked points. Mark off one section onto a piece of white card. Draw in on card pattern for one section of side, using same glass as guide for loop, and straight parallel lines drawn with ruler to within one inch of lower edge for swags between the loops. (These lines will each exactly fit one of the creases.) Now trace off this pattern from the card section by section, moving the strip along, and fasten round the cake with a pin through the ½-inch overlap. Using a fine skewer prick out both patterns on top of

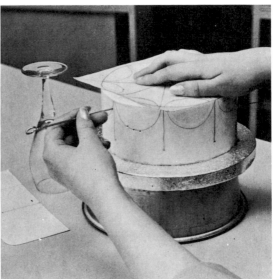

cake and round sides, making sure the two patterns fit together. Remove templates.

Pipe in with Gelatine Icing and a No. 2 writing tube, the side and top loops and swags with line piping, the base with spaced-out blobs; the top loops are then over-piped with dots, more dots are piped between and on top of the blobs, and two dots where sections meet. Moulded marzipan raspberries

are placed round the edge of the cake where the side and top loops meet. (See on p. 32 how to make them.)

## ICING TECHNIQUES

**Royal Icing:** The most common fault is to leave bubbles in the icing. On the top of the cake, smooth the icing out from the centre to the edge in circular swirls with a palette knife, working the icing to and fro, to eliminate bubbles. After smoothing across with the ruler, remove surplus icing from top edge by drawing the knife round the cake, as if icing the sides, and return surplus icing to bowl. (Remember only to uncover bowl to remove or return icing.) Allow top to dry. For the sides, take small quantities of icing on the palette knife and apply to the sides of the cake vertically. Again, smooth the icing to and fro to remove bubbles, and work round the sides until completely covered. Remove any surplus icing from top edge with a knife and return to mixing bowl. When icing a square cake, follow the same method, but ice two opposite sides first, remove surplus icing, allow to dry, then ice the other two opposite sides. When all are dry, a piece of very fine sandpaper can be used to smooth away any rough edges.

**Glacé Icing:** The difficulty here is to cover smoothly, and prevent cracking when the icing is dry. Sides should be straightened by filling in with butter cream or smearing in a little of the icing stiffened with added icing sugar, before you begin. Place cake on wire tray over a plate to catch icing drips. Pour the icing exactly onto the centre of the cake all at once. Tilt the wire tray to help the icing to flow evenly, only touching it with the palette knife if absolutely necessary. Any icing left in the bowl is usually needed to fill in the sides near the base where the cake is not completely coated. Transfer cake to serving plate before icing sets, and press decorations lightly into place, as decorating or moving the cake may cause cracking once the icing has become completely set.

**Butter Cream:** All uncooked icings including butter or margarine are comparatively easy to apply because they will stand handling, and can be smoothed over if the first attempt at decorating is not successful. Do not attempt to get a smooth surface, as this is very difficult with butter cream, and it can be marked in so many decorative patterns. The cake should be placed on an upturned plate or turn-table to ice. If the top only is to be iced, you may find it helpful to pin a greaseproof paper "collar" round the sides of the cake and spread the icing inside this. The same method can be used for glacé icing, but although it keeps the sides of the cake clean, it tends to tear away the edge of the icing when removed, even with extreme care.

## HOW TO USE A TURN-TABLE

If you are interested in icing designs and carrying them out accurately, you will soon appreciate how much easier it is to do this using a turn-table. The more expensive models which can be adjusted to any height are heavy and rather expensive, but a smaller, light one made of tin or plastic (see photograph on p. 8) will serve the purpose if you raise it on books, bricks or block of wood to a convenient working height. An inexpensive plastic model has storage grooves for piping syringe and tubes in the top, and thus serves a dual purpose.

To cover the side of a round cake evenly the best method is to turn the table while holding the knife against the side of the cake (impossible without a turn-table) and when marking out a design through a template it is a great time saver. Experiment until you find a comfortable working height. Generally speaking, this will be (when standing to ice top of cake) so that top edge of cake comes level with your elbows. When sitting (to ice sides of cake) when top of turn-table comes level with your elbows.

# Making Separate Sugar Decorations

BESIDES the decorations which are piped straight onto the cake itself, there are others which can be made separately, dried off, and then attached to the cake with icing. Of these, the easiest and prettiest you can make are piped sugar flowers. They are best made of royal icing, well beaten so that the icing stands in peaks in the mixing bowl when lifted with a spoon. A few drops of acetic acid should be added as this makes the icing set more firmly and, if required, food colourings to tint the icing to the appropriate shade for the flower you are copying. According to the size of flower you want, use No. 11 or 42 flat petal tubes, or for roses, No. 18 or 36 curved petal tubes. Raised flowers are piped on to a pick, which is removed when they are dry; flat flowers are piped onto waxed paper, and eased off with a palette knife when dry. Of the raised flowers, roses are the most popular.

**How to pipe sugar roses:** (See example on p. 38). Make up a small batch of royal icing as described above and if liked tint pink. To make them more realistic, have two batches of icing and two piping bags, with different shades of icing. For instance, use deep pink for the centre of the roses, and pale pink for the outer petals. Hold the small stick or pick in your left hand with the tube held against the upper end of the stick, and pipe round it three times to form the centre of the rose. Practise twirling the stick in the opposite direction as you force out the icing until you get the "feel" of this movement. Now make three fairly tight petals round the bud. Beginning each time at the base, pipe a semi-circle of icing, finishing off the petal and beginning the next overlapping it as you turn the stick. (If using two shades of icing, change to the lighter shade now.) Pipe three to five more petals, with a more open movement so that the edges turn back more, always overlapping a new petal over the last one, and turning the stick to get a free, easy movement.

When the flower looks large enough, put the stick holding it into the pick board so that it rests holding the flower clear of the board. If the flower seems top-heavy on one side, you can slant the pick to correct this

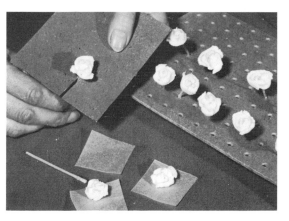

British Sugar Corporation

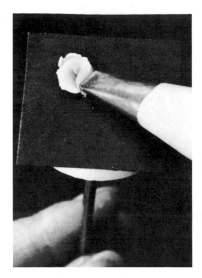

till it dries. When the flowers are quite dry (overnight if possible) remove onto grease-proof paper by running the stick down the slit in a piece of cardboard, as described on p. 10, and easing out the stick. The rose will be left resting on the cardboard; slide it carefully onto a sheet of greaseproof paper so as not to damage it.

Make as many roses as you require for the decoration, which you will have planned out in advance, and make a few extras to allow for breakages in handling. If the design calls for some buds, finish them off without adding the five open petals.

Flat piped flowers are easier to make, if rather less effective than roses. Among these, narcissi, pansies and forget-me-nots are favourites.

**How to pipe sugar narcissi:** (See example on p. 59). Work each flower individually on a small square of waxed paper fixed onto an icing nail. The nails have plastic heads about twice the size of a drawing pin, fixed to a spike like a thin skewer. While piping fix the waxed paper to the head of the nail with a dab of icing. Again, use stiff royal icing with a drop or two of acetic acid added. Using a small petal tube and plain white icing, pipe the first petal using a semi-circular movement, turning the icing nail slowly in the opposite direction. Pipe six petals altogether to complete the circle of the flower. After three petals have been piped, an exact half-circle should have been made. Now pipe a complete circle on top of the petals to form the centre of the flower. Make as many as required plus a few spares. Allow flowers to dry completely before removing from the paper. When dry, paint the centres yellow with a clean paint brush and saffron food colouring. Use the end of a palette knife (heated if you experience difficulty) to remove flowers. Lift into position on cake with tweezers.

Very simple flat flowers with four, five or more petals look quite effective done in any delicate pastel colour, provided the petals are all piped in neatly to the centre. The flowers can be placed in groups of three, or used as a wreath border to a square or circle filled in with piped trellis work, or to surround medallions on the side of a cake.

**How to make moulded roses:** Quite large and most realistic flowers, especially roses, can be moulded from almond or Satin Icing Paste, or Plastic or Fondant Icing. Begin by working sufficient food colouring into the paste to colour as required. (The roses shown in the Flower Basket Cake which features on p. 89 were tinted apricot with equal quantities of saffron yellow and cochineal.) Knead paste until colour is evenly distributed. Following the stages from top left to lower right of the photograph, begin by working a small piece of paste with the fingers until it is a suitable petal shape. Roll to make centre of the rose. To make the rest of the petals, work the paste into thin rose-petal shapes as for the first petal. Place one petal on either side of the moulded centre, furling closely round it. Work five more petals and overlap round the other two. The completed rose should have seven overlapping petals. Cut off any excess paste at the base with a pair of scissors. Allow to dry thoroughly on a piece of waxed paper before placing them in position on the cake.

If you would like to add leaves and stems to your roses, tint some of the paste with sap green colouring. Roll out thinly. Cut a strip with a curved inner edge and the outer edge cut in five sharp points for the calyx. Wrap round the base of the rose, and turn back the points slightly. Using a real rose leaf (or picture) as guide for shape, cut out leaves in proportion to the size of your

British Sugar Corporation

Colour and mould into fruits as required. When dry, paint with edible food colourings if necessary.

**Raspberries:** Tint some of the paste deep pink. Tint a very small quantity bright green. Form tiny balls of the pink paste into the shape of a raspberry, mark all over with the point of fine skewer. Roll tiny spikes of green paste and press into base of fruit, at stalk end.

**Oranges and lemons:** Tint some of the paste orange and some yellow. Form the orange paste into round balls, mark all over close together lightly with skewer and indent deeply at one point. Form the yellow paste into slightly more oval shapes for lemons, and finish as for oranges. Paint in stalk end with green food colouring.

**Pears:** Tint some of the paste very pale green and form into tiny pear shapes. Trim cloves to make suitable sized stalk and base for pears. If liked, paint one side of the pears with pink food colouring to imitate the skins of ripe pears.

**Bananas:** Tint some of the paste yellow. Form into tiny banana shapes, making one flat side, and two parallel ridges on top coming together at each end of the fruit. Paint in lines along these ridges with brown food colouring and dots at either end.

If preferred, fruits (and vegetables) can be moulded from almond paste, and then painted with food colourings, instead of kneading the colourings into the paste. If you enjoy painting, this delicate work can be most interesting. Do not aim to get all the items in true relation to their natural sizes (for example, a marzipan orange much larger than the raspberry) but roughly all the same size. When moulding vegetables it is a convention to show half a split pea pod with the peas resting in this open half. Potatoes are moulded as roughly shaped balls with a few

moulded flowers. Mark in the veins and serrate the edges. Roll out very thin "ropes" of the paste for stalks.

Another form of decoration can be made by moulding fruit, or even vegetables, from almond paste (see Raspberry Layer Cake on p. 27).

## BASIC PASTE FOR MARZIPAN FRUITS

*1 lb. loaf sugar; ¼ pt. water; large pinch cream of tartar; 4 oz. fine semolina; 8 oz. ground almonds; 2 egg whites, lightly beaten; few drops* EACH, *almond and vanilla essence; 4 oz. sieved icing sugar.*

Slowly dissolve loaf sugar in water. Add cream of tartar. Bring to boil and boil till mixture forms a soft ball when dropped in cold water (240° F., if using a sugar thermometer). Remove from heat and stir briskly till syrup becomes grainy and opaque. Beat in fine semolina, almonds, egg whites and flavourings, then work in sieved icing sugar. Knead till smooth and cold on a slab or board, dusted with sieved icing sugar.

**Above—Party Chicks: each one is made from a small round of sponge cut into three; a chart shows you how on p. 101**

Kraft Foods

**Below—Iced Butterfly Cake: rectangle of chocolate cake makes this realistic butterfly; full instructions on p. 88**

Cadbury Typhoo Food Advisory Service

Left—Chocolate Éclairs: the classic choice for afternoon tea, based on delicate choux pastry and filled with whipped cream

McDougalls Cookery Service

Right — Christmas Stars : baked in star-shaped tins are easy to ice and pipe with a fancy border to emphasise the basic shape

Cadbury Typhoo Food Advisory Service

Plate 4

**Right—Kentucky Nut Cake:** the nutty flavour of the cake contrasts well with a velvet smooth topping which demonstrates an easy finish any amateur could copy

Cadbury Typhoo Food Advisory Service

**Left—Bavarian Coffee Torte:** the dark cake is seen through a lattice work of cream, and the edge is bordered with quartered glacé cherries

Modern Woman

Plate 5

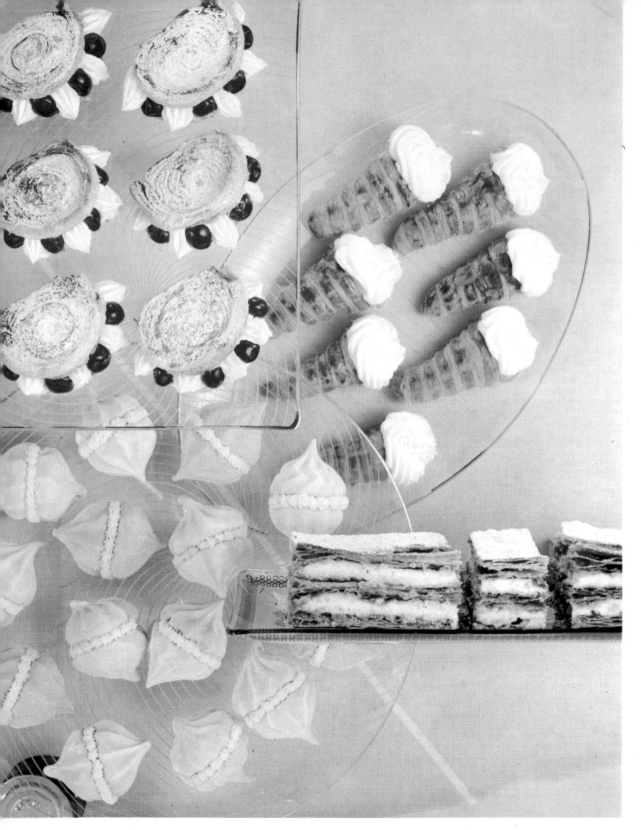

Nestlé's Cookery Service

**Afternoon Tea Pastries: a spectacular assortment of the best loved favourites,
Cream Horns, Cream Crisps, Cream Slices and Meringues in pastel shades**

Plate 6

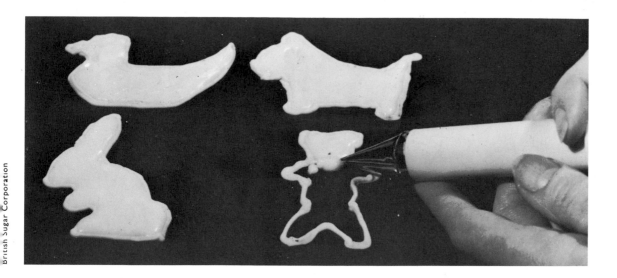

indentations only, then rolled in cocoa.

Another form of decoration is the run-in "plaque", or flat shape specially useful for applying to the sides of a cake.

**How to make plaques:** They are usually made in a colour that contrasts with the icing of the cake so that it shows up well. (See the example of plaques in the shape of pink hearts on p. 60.) There are several ways of making these, but the simplest way for the beginner is to draw round the shape of a fancy cutter on white card. For a child's party cake animal cutters would be particularly suitable. Above, we show four easily recognised shapes—a duck, a dog, a rabbit and bear. A sheet of waxed paper twice the width of the card on which the shapes have been drawn is laid over it, so that the upper left hand corners of both card and waxed paper match. The paper is anchored to the card by four tiny dabs of icing. Now, using a No. 1 writing tube and fairly firm glacé icing tinted the required colour, pipe over the outlines of the animals. While these dry, slide the paper across, anchor again with icing, and trace out another set of animals. (You will now have a set of eight tracings.) Thin the icing slightly, so that it will flow

readily, and using a larger tube or a grease-proof paper bag with a small diagonal snipped off the end, fill in the whole outline. This process is called "flooding". Use the rounded blade of a knife or a blunt skewer to help the icing into the corners of the pattern, taking care not to overrun the edge. Allow to dry out at least overnight, or longer. Now with a No. 1 writing tube pipe in any details you wish, such as dots for the eyes, a collar for the dog, etc., and leave again to dry. With scissors, cut into squares each containing one animal. To remove from the paper, place the square of paper close to and parallel with the edge of the table. Slide out paper over edge until one-third of animal protrudes past edge of table, begin to peel back the paper under it, supporting the body of the plaque flat on the table with the fingers of the other hand. Gradually ease paper away until half the animal is released, reverse so that free side is resting on table with paper pressed back against edge. Ease this half of the paper away, sliding plaque back onto table-top as you do this. (If set really hard before the paper is removed, there is little danger of the plaques breaking, but do not be tempted to try it too soon). The plaques can be easily attached to the sides of a square cake but should not be more than an inch wide for a round cake, or they will not fit round the shape of the cake. After some experience you can attempt quite complicated designs, For example figures of children, circus animals and clowns, or fairytale characters, can be traced from a book onto white card, the outlines piped over this, then flooded, and the details copied with a No. 1 writing tube and different coloured icings from the original pictures when the plaque is dry.

The type of almond paste recommended for moulding fruits, and also stiff Satin Icing Paste, are suitable for patchwork icing.

**How to make patchwork icing:** Use an embroidery transfer with a central figure or group of figures, or perhaps a cottage, for the top of the cake, and smaller details of the transfer such as flowers or small animals to go round the sides. Tint the almond paste at least four different colours, such as pink (for faces and hands) brown (for hair, shoes, etc.) and two bright colours for clothing. If a cottage scene is chosen you will need brown for roof, fence, etc., green for foliage, and two pastel shades for· flowers. Roll out each piece of paste very thinly. Cut up the transfer, place each piece pattern-wise on the appropriate coloured paste and cut round it with a sharp knife. (Keep board, rolling pin and hands dusted lightly with cornflour during the process.) Brush surface of icing with a thin layer of egg white, and assemble the pieces of the pattern. Allow to dry off overnight. With a fine paint brush and brown food colouring, paint in details, such as features on faces and folds of clothing, panes in cottage windows, and so on. Piped flowers can be worked into these designs. Two-toned ones are especially realistic.

**How to make two-toned flowers:** Raised flowers piped round picks or flat-piped on waxed paper can be given shaded petals. To make pansies, fill the syringe or icing bag with a large spoonful of yellow tinted icing placed in one side, and a large spoonful of mauve tinted icing in the other. As you adjust the plunger or turn down the top of the bag, the two lots of icing will come together, and after testing to make sure both colours are flowing out of the tube, you can flat-pipe the pansies, using the same method as for narcissi, making five petals only. When the flowers are dry, pipe a group of dots with icing tinted a stronger shade of yellow, and a No. 1 writing tube, in the centre, and draw out a few short lines with brown food colouring and a fine paint brush a little way from the centre to edge. To make a wild rose, line the icing bag with white icing and fill centre with pale pink icing, make five petals and finish with yellow centres as for pansies.

Leaves to go with piped flowers can also be piped out flat onto waxed paper with icing tinted green and leaf tube No. 17, or No. 10 for larger leaves. Draw the point of the tube away sharply to make raised leaves. Pipe plenty so you need only use the best shaped ones.

**Bought cake decorations:** The most useful are silver dragées in the shape of balls, to place on piped rosettes elaborating simple decorative piping, or close together in rows to make patterns, such as stars, or spell out words. Avoid putting them in place until the icing is nearly dry, or they may sink in. If, on the other hand, the icing is completely dry, it may crack when placing the silver balls. Mimosa balls, resembling fluffy yellow mimosa flowers in size and appearance, come in other colours besides yellow. Piped sugar flowers also come in white and pastel shades, but do not always blend happily with your own piping. Non-edible decorations include miniature green and silver leaves, silver bells and horseshoes, and candle holders of all sizes and colours.

# Piping Decorations

THE consistency of the icing used for piping is most important and makes all the difference between a neatly finished cake with clear designs, and a messy, disappointing result.

Royal icing is generally best for piping, as glacé icing is inclined to run and will not hold its shape so well. The icing should be like very thick cream, which will pull up with a wooden spoon into soft points. If the icing sugar has been well sieved, the icing is well beaten before use and has not been allowed to form a crust, the tubes will not clog. However, the tiniest lump can clog the end of a tube and spoil the pattern which emerges or even block up the tube completely. Do not try to force out or pry out the lump or you may injure the tube. Remove it, wash out and dry thoroughly, replace it and then carry on.

**Flooding:** There is one type of decoration where glacé icing is suitable, and that is for flooding a large area in a contrasting colour, inside a piped design on top of a cake. The area may be circular, square, or star-shaped. (In the photograph below you see four circles.) The area is marked out round a plain or fancy cutter, pricked out through a template, or round a pattern cut in thick paper. The shape is then piped in in outline with a writing or star tube. This area is then flooded with soft glacé icing (or soft royal icing) through a paper icing bag as for making plaques, and gently persuaded to fill the pattern completely. The border can be over-piped with rosettes if the writing tube was used in the first instance, or masked with sugar flowers, or over-piped with simple dots. Over-piping (which will be discussed later in this chapter) should only be done when the flooded decoration is quite dry.

## EXPERIMENTS IN PIPING

Begin to practise with the tubes you will use most, the star and writing tubes.

**How to use star tubes:** Star (or rose) tubes come in a great variety of sizes and designs. For instance, there is a 4-pointed star tube,

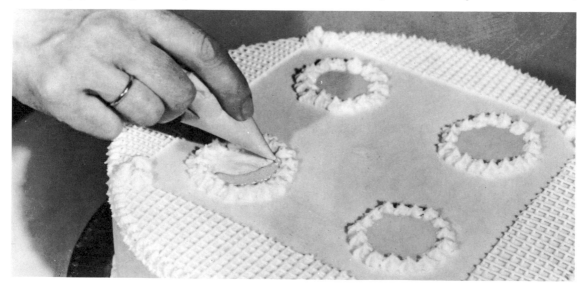

1.

2.

3.

4.

5.

British Sugar Corporation

and do not require such a confident and steady touch.

In the photograph on the left you can see a number of patterns all made with an 8-pointed star tube. Here is how they and others are made.

Always work from left to right, or towards you, holding bag at a steep angle.

1. Start half an inch above the line along which the border is to run. Pipe down and then along that line for about half an inch, releasing pressure and lifting tube sharply. Begin half an inch below the line, just left of the tail of the first scroll, pipe up and inwards to cover it then along the line for half an inch. Repeat the scrolls alternately from above and below.

2. Begin piping along the line of the border for half an inch, move the bag up and anti-clockwise in a tight "e" shape, then down to the line and along it for another half an inch; then make another "e". This piping makes a continuous border which can be varied by lengthening the space between the "e"-shaped loops.

3. Begin to pipe out a rosette on the line of the border, move the bag along the line, upwards and in a tight loop anti-clockwise, then return to the line and finish off by releasing pressure and lifting tube sharply.

4. Make oval or lozenge-shaped scrolls which can be used as a continuous border. Begin on the line of the border and make a con-tinuous "e" pattern, each "e" partially cover-ing the one behind it, exerting more pressure and widening the sweep of the movement towards the centre of the scroll, lightening the pressure and reducing sweep as you finish it.

5. Rosettes or stars are made holding the bag vertically on top, or horizontally if working against the side of the cake. Place tube close to surface of cake, press and pull away quickly to form a neat rosette well pointed up in the centre.

Other ways to use star tubes will be de-

small and large 6-pointed star tubes, 8, 10 and 12-pointed star tubes, and a fancy star tube. Naturally you cannot produce tiny, delicate rosettes with a large star tube, but if from this selection you choose one large and one small, you will be able to achieve all the designs shown in this book calling for star tubes, although your results may look a little different from the cakes photographed. That is one of the delights of pipe work; by using different tubes from those suggested, you may achieve even prettier effects. Practise with these first before attempting to use the writing tubes as on the whole star tubes are easier to manage for the beginner,

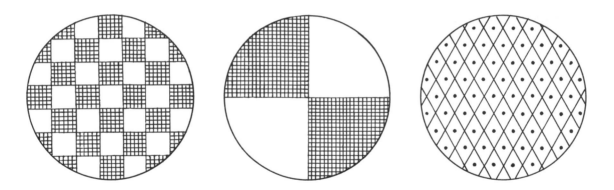

monstrated later in the book. You will also see shell borders, and doubled borders made with shell tubes (flat one side, serrated the other) or with star tubes. Shells are made by beginning as for a rosette, carrying tube a fraction back and away from you and bringing over and towards you again, releasing pressure and drawing away tube. Each shell is piped just to cover the tail of the last one. A continuous border is made by "doubling" the tube, moving it in a straight line forward, but hesitating every inch to move the tube back a quarter of an inch and then forward again.

Practise these patterns on an upturned plate, well washed and dried, if possible one with a base the same size as the cake you are going to decorate. Or invert the cake tin on your turn-table, and practise on the top and sides of the tin. The icing can be scraped off and returned to the bowl before it sets, and used again for practice. Begin holding the tube close to, but not touching, the surface, at a very slight angle from the vertical, except for rosettes. Start with simple scroll designs, both continuous and separate patterns. When you have mastered the art of exerting and relaxing pressure as you pipe out the icing, turn to practice with writing tubes.

**How to use writing tubes:** The other most popular tube is the writer, but this requires a steady hand to manipulate correctly. It comes in three sizes, of which No. 1 is the finest, and No. 3 the heaviest. In the photograph below you see examples of the kind of work done with a No. 2 writing tube. Apart from writing messages of greeting in script, long-hand and Roman lettering, these tubes are most used for trellis work. This consists of rows of parallel lines set close together, and then over-piped at right angles. Above are sketches of three very simple ways to decorate the top of a round cake with trellis. The first and second use square trellis, the third is covered in diagonal trellis, which is made by crossing the first set of lines diagonally instead of at right angles. A dot placed in the centre of each diamond makes it appear an elaborate pattern, but it is really very simple. So are line-and-dot borders as shown here, and scrolls in the shape of an "s" turned backwards onto its side.

Now we are ready to see how other tubes are used, and how separately made sugar

British Sugar Corporation

37

roses are used as part of a design piped onto the cake.

**How to decorate a wedding cake:** This 2-tier White Rose Wedding Cake was made on the base of the one-stage fruit cakes (see recipe p. 122). The decorations were entirely made of sugar, all in white. Two tubes only were used for piping, No. 1 writing tube and No. 20 fine rope tube. The roses and leaves were made separately with No. 36 petal tube and No. 17 leaf tube.

The tops of the two cakes were divided into semi-circles along the sides, and fan shapes at the corners, by pricking out round segments of circles of different sizes. (Saucers were used as guides.) The circle on top of the smaller cake was drawn round a plain cutter. The cakes were both mounted on square silver boards large enough to allow a wide border, which was covered with a maze of squiggles using the No. 1 writing tube. Pink velvet ribbon was fixed round the edges of both boards. The shapes on top of both cakes were outlined with the No. 1 writing tube, then filled in with trellis. The outlines, the top edges and bases of both cakes were finished with very fine doubled borders using the No. 20 fine rope tube. Separately made white sugar roses, each flanked by two leaves, were positioned with dabs of icing on the corners of both cakes, and more sugar roses in the centre of each side of the larger cake. A group of roses and leaves was placed in the centre of the top tier.

A design was created for the sides, each side showing one full looped garland (shown in sketch below) in the centre, flanked by two half-garlands. These were joined at the corners to give the effect of continuous loops all round each cake. The garlands on the smaller cake were less elaborate but repeated the same theme. They were made up of line piping with the No. 1 tube, forget-me-nots piped with the same tube in a ring of five dots with one dot in the centre, and the leaves and roses affixed with dabs of icing.

Four square pillars were positioned on the lower tier by placing corners of pillars to centre of each fan design. Top tier was supported by these pillars.

NOTE: The same saucers used as guides for decorating tops of cakes were used to produce paper templates for side decorations. Notice how the curve of each garland balances an opposite curve on top of the cake, producing a harmonious and pleasing pattern.

**Stages in piping a 2-tier wedding cake:** (See Silver Bells Wedding Cake on Colour Plate No. 2). The basic cakes were made from the Fruit Cake Mixture No. 1 (see p. 120), and decorated with piping and artificial ornaments. Three tubes were used, No. 2 writing tube, No. 6 star tube and No. 12 shell tube.

A square of paper was cut and folded to mark diagonals the same length as diameter of large cake (8-inch square of paper for 11-inch round cake). This was laid on top of the cake so that all four points touched the edge, and point where diagonals crossed secured with a pin to mark centre of cake. The pattern was pricked out with a fine skewer round this square. The top of the smaller cake was completely covered with trellis, using No. 2 writing tube. See in the photograph how this is begun with a straight line across the centre of the cake and worked out to the edge, then worked out from this central line to the other edge, to ensure that lines remain parallel. On large areas of trellis work this is important. Trellis pattern was filled in all round the square on the lower tier, being careful to keep lines in every section of design parallel with other sections. Four round pillars were positioned 1½ inches in from the corners of the square with dabs of icing, and as each was placed in position the edge was masked with rosettes, using the No. 6 star tube. (Providing the trellis has been allowed to set completely first this will not be disturbed, and the method of work-

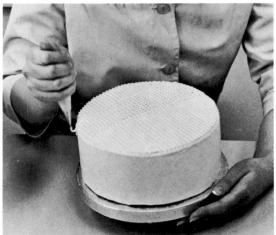

ing follows the general rule of working from the centre outwards whenever possible.)

A border of rosettes was piped round top edge of both cakes and another similar border immediately against this on the sides of the cakes. This type of finish conceals any irregularities in the edges. Both cakes were positioned on silver boards with dabs of icing, and the bases of the cakes finished with shell edging using No. 12 shell tube. The artificial silver leaves, horse shoes and bells were secured with dabs and rosettes of icing, and the top tier placed on the lower tier.
NOTE: It is most important when icing an elaborate tiered cake to finish each stage while it is easiest to get access to the surface to be piped without damaging the work already done. As I have just shown, the best way is to work from the centre outwards whenever possible, and to allow each stage of piping to dry out completely before proceeding to the next.

**How to make raised lattice baskets:** Although these really come under the heading of separately made sugar decorations, they are dealt with here, because they require some considerable skill and practice in using the writing tube, and should only be made after you have learned how to pipe neat trellis patterns straight onto the cake. The baskets

are made by piping trellis in various ways onto a shaped mould, removing when dry. The three shapes of net nail (as these moulds are called) most commonly used are the oval, border and pyramid. If you have no net nails, simple baskets can be piped on the backs of bun tins or on the backs of boat-shaped patty tins.

The basic method is always the same. Grease the net nail or back of the tin very lightly with lard. Holding the nail or side of tin with your left hand, pipe square or diagonal trellis all over it, using a No. 1 or 2 writing tube, and firm royal icing. To make smaller baskets, cover the shape only half-way down the mould, or make two baskets

on the one nail at the same time using, for example, two adjacent sides of the pyramid nail for each basket (see p. 62, the Basket-trimmed Wedding Cake).

Turn and tilt the nail as necessary, but make all the joins and edge finishes very neat and firm. If this is difficult when using boat-shaped patty tins, mount the tins by running a thin skewer into a cork, and fixing each tin, as you pipe it, inverted on top of the cork with a dab of icing. Either finish the edge of the basket with a strong border of line piping (which can be masked with rosettes when the basket has been fixed to the cake) or finish the basket itself with a border of rosettes using a star tube.

The oval net nail can be used in various ways. Cover completely, and you have a deep firm basket which, if over-piped with basket weave is strong enough to fill with sweets. Cover only one side of the oval to make a shallow open basket to set against the side of a cake. Or cover the top entirely but bring the trellis only half-way down the sides of the mould to make a closed oval shape to put on top of a cake.

The border nail is used to make a shape which fits over the edge of the cake, part resting on top and part against the side of the cake. It is the most difficult to remove from the nail without breaking but perhaps the most spectacular in effect.

As the baskets are completed, press the point of the nail into a sheet of thick cork, or through the shallow lid of a cardboard box and leave for about 48 hours to dry. It may be possible to ease them off the nails with the point of a knife without any difficulty if they have been kept in a warm room; but if they tend to stick, warm slightly in a very mild heat, such as a slightly warm oven, or if using tin moulds, by holding a lighted candle under the mould for a minute or so. As the baskets are fragile, do make several more than are needed. Remember that if you are short of even one basket when you come to finish the cake, you cannot hasten the process of drying out, and will have to make more baskets and wait another 48 hours before completing the decoration.

**How to apply lattice baskets:** The position for the baskets will be marked in on the cake as part of the design. To secure a basket on top of the cake, put it in the marked position and anchor with two pins stuck vertically through the basket and into the icing, so that it will not move while the join is masked with piped rosettes. If the edge is already finished with rosettes it should be lightly smeared underneath with wet icing so that the basket adheres when applied to the cake. To affix baskets to the side of a cake, it will always be necessary to anchor with pins driven through it horizontally into the cake, to take the weight of the basket until the icing used to attach it has dried and the pins can be carefully withdrawn.

**How to pipe basket-weave:** This very effective form of decoration can be done in two ways. The two-toned weave requires two tubes. Below is shown the simple basket-weave. You need only one tube, No. 9 fancy band tube, and one shade of icing. Pipe in stages, alternately vertical then horizontal, as shown in the sketches below, to cover the entire area to be piped. Work from left to right. On a simple round cake it is easier to finish the top first, then do the sides. Pipe a straight vertical down from top to bottom, starting at right of area to be piped. Cross it with horizontals leaving a space the same width as the band itself between them, and

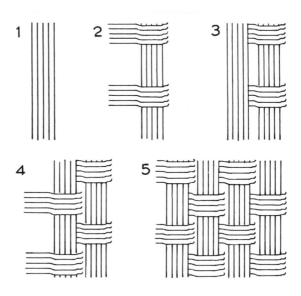

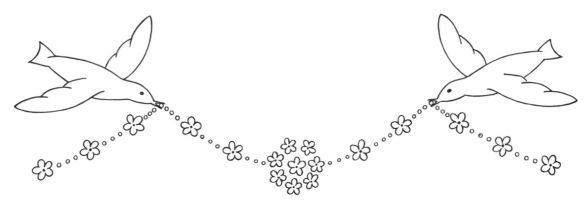

extending them the same distance out to the left of the vertical. Pipe another vertical over these protruding ends. Now pipe another set of horizontals beginning in the spaces which you left vacant last time.

**Other uses for writing tubes:** The fine No. 1 writing tube is perhaps the most versatile of all, because it easily produces both lines and dots, which can be very tiny, or larger if pressure is harder and more prolonged. The simplest garland pattern, which is really a series of loops, can be made by piping a forget-me-not head every half-inch or so, and filling in the spaces between them with tiny dots. To give weight to the garland, make a central arrangement of buds or leaves as well as flower heads so that it appears natural. The loops of the garland can be supported by outlines of blue-birds, as shown in the sketch above, or true-lovers-knots, or actual tiny ribbon bows, fixed with dabs of icing.

Experience will make you adept with the writing tubes, but although dots are made at the same angle as rosettes, lines must be drawn at a slight angle. Let the tube touch the cake at the commencement of the movement only, then lift tube away from cake slowly and steadily as you exert pressure and draw out the line of icing to the required shape and distance. When the movement is completed cease pressure, drop point of tube back onto cake to break the thread and lift again quickly. Do not let the thread touch the surface of the cake in the middle of any movement, or the shape will be spoilt. The writing of words should always be practised over pencilled writing on greaseproof paper to give confidence before piping onto the cake. The writing tubes are also useful for over-piping. A design can be given depth and sharpness by being over-piped with any tube of smaller diameter than the first (larger tubes would be top-heavy) and professionally made cakes are often over-piped two or three times to create a rich effect, each time with a more delicate tube, and usually finishing with No. 1 writing tube in matching or contrasting colour. The difficulty is to avoid having the over-piping slip to one side or the other of the pattern, which gives a lop-sided effect, and a very steady hand is needed.

**Terms used to describe icing techniques:** If you are following a new recipe, you may not understand what is meant by such terms as *cording, scrolling, coiling, doubling* and *shaking* the tubes. Cording is done by covering a simple line with close dots; scrolling or coiling by moving the tube in a series of close, anti-clockwise "e" shapes; doubling by a check hesitation and slight backwards movement of the tube before continuing forward every inch or half-inch; shaking, by moving the tube forwards in a zig-zag pattern from side to side.

# Christmas Cakes

OST housewives enjoy making and also decorating their own Christmas cakes, even if they cannot spare the time for it at any other season of the year.

## CHRISTMAS LANTERN CAKE

*Make up Fruit Cake Mixture No. 1 (see p. 120) in 9 × 5 × 3-inch tin, quantities as for 8-inch round tin.*

Make up 1 lb. almond paste. Trim sides and ends of cake perpendicular and stand cake upright. Mark the centre point on the top end and mark a line 3 inches from the point on each side. With a sharp knife, cut away the four top edges, working from the centre point and trimming outwards to the marked line to form a roof shape.

Cut off about a third of the almond paste. Roll out the larger portion on sugared paper and cut a strip 5 inches wide, long enough to go round the cake. Cut also 4 triangles for the top sections. Brush cake with warmed jam and fit into position. Leave for 24 hours to become firm.

Knead sufficient gravy browning into the remaining almond paste to give a deep colour. Roll out and cut 4 strips 4 inches long and 1 inch wide and a 1-inch strip long enough to go round the base of the lantern. Brush the strips with warmed jam and fit the long one round the base. Press the short strips lengthwise down each corner, allowing $\frac{1}{2}$ inch to project on each side. Cut 8 strips $\frac{1}{4}$ inch wide, and 4 triangles for the top sections as before. Brush the strips with jam and arrange 2 at right angles on each side to form "panes".

Cut up half a packet of strawberry table

jelly in small pieces and melt over a low heat with one teaspoonful water, taking care that it does not burn. Pour a little jelly into each "pane" with a teaspoon, spreading with a knife. Allow each side to set firm before turning over to do the next. When quite set, brush the triangles with jam and fit on to the top sections. Leave overnight.

Put the cake on a 6-inch square board and apply a little butter cream roughly to the top to represent snow. Soften a 4-inch strip of angelica in hot water, bend into a loop and fix to the top with butter cream. Decorate corners of board with holly leaves.

**Christmas Lantern Cake: a realistic and most effective Lantern, with shining red panes easily made from a strawberry jelly**

McDougalls Cookery Service

43

**Raisin Chocolate Log: a rich cake in the Continental tradition where the subtle flavours of chestnut, chocolate and rum are mingled with plump raisins**

## RAISIN CHOCOLATE LOG CAKE

*Make a 4-egg chocolate swiss roll (see p. 125) in an 8 × 12-inch tin.*

Filling and icing ingredients:

*4 oz. California seedless raisins; 2 tablespoonfuls rum; 16 oz. tin sweetened chestnut purée; 2 oz. butter; 4 oz. icing sugar.*

To make the filling, place the raisins in a saucepan and pour over the rum. Bring to the boil and leave to stand until cold. Beat together the chestnut purée, butter and icing sugar until smooth and creamy. Divide mixture in half and add raisins to one half of the mixture. Unroll the sponge gently and remove the paper, as described in the recipe on p. 125. Spread with the raisin filling, and

roll up again tightly. Cut one end off diagonally and attach to side of log to represent a branch. Cover the roll completely with the remaining chestnut cream, smooth neatly and fork lines along length of cake to represent bark. Smooth edge of cut branch and pipe on a spiral of white glacé icing with a fine writing tube. Decorate by sprinkling with icing sugar through a sieve, and with miniature holly leaves or a robin ornament.

This cake appeals particularly to those who like a rich cake with the traditional look of Christmas, but who do not like almond paste or hard icing. It can be kept for several days before cutting, and is in fact another version of the French Chocolate Log Cake which should be eaten soon after it is made.

## CHRISTMAS PRESENT CAKES

*Make up Fruit Cake Mixture No. 1 (see p. 120). Divide mixture evenly between 3 5-inch round tins, bake in a moderate oven for ½ an hour, reduce to a cool oven for a further 1¼ hours. Cover tops and sides of all 3 cakes in usual way with almond paste, ½ lb. for each.*

Rough ice one cake and tie a red ribbon round it. Here are two other suggestions.

### Diamond Christmas Cake

You will need ½ lb. royal icing. Coat top and sides, mount with dab of icing on 7-inch silver board, ice to edge of board. Draw an icing comb round sides evenly. Mark diamond pattern with a skewer on top. With a fine writing tube pipe scrolls round top edge of cake and against bottom edge. Over-pipe scrolls in green icing, and with a larger writing tube pipe dots on all points of diamonds and under edging scrolls at base.

### "A Happy Christmas" Cake

You will need ½ lb. royal icing. Coat top and sides, mount cake on 7-inch board and ice to edge. With a fine star tube pipe stars round top and lower edges of cake, using pink icing. Repeat star design round base in two circles, piping outside circle alternately with the inside. Decorate sides and outer ring of board with dots, using a fine writing tube. Pipe "A HAPPY CHRISTMAS" on top with this tube, then over-pipe in white.

**Christmas Present Cakes: just the gift for a small family, and you can make all three from one batch of fruit cake mixture**

Butter Information Council

## DUTCH CHRISTMAS ROSE CAKE

Here is a cake that's really different, with a special recipe and a decoration you can store and use again another year.

*Make up Fruit Cake Mixture No. 1 (see p. 120) in an 8-inch round tin using Dutch unsalted butter. Cool, prick with skewer and pour over a wineglassful of rum.*

Make $1\frac{1}{2}$ lb. almond paste and cover cake in the usual way. Reserve a little almond paste to make the holly leaves and berries, wrapped in foil to keep it moist. Make $1\frac{1}{2}$ lb. royal icing, ice as for the Nowell Christmas Cake (see p. 47) reserving a teacupful of icing in a closely covered container, and mount with a dab of icing on a 10-inch board. Put reserved icing into a basin.

To make the centre decoration, sprinkle on a coffeespoonful of gum tragacanth (obtainable from the chemist), stir well until it forms a stiff paste. Mould five small thin petals for each flower, arrange over the top

**Above—Dutch Christmas Rose Cake:** this design features a decoration you can make yourself and save to use again, resembling a wreath of dainty Christmas roses surrounding a candle in the centre

Dutch Dairy Bureau

**Right—Christmas Parcel Cake:** for those who do not enjoy working out an elaborate and formal design this cake has a nicely decorative look; the flat icing used is very easy to handle and gives a smooth finish to the cake's surface

Cadbury Typhoo Food Advisory Service

of a capped bottle sticking the petals together, overlapping each other, with egg white. Allow petals to fall naturally to resemble a Christmas rose, leave to set. Reverse each flower into a small cup of foil whilst another flower is being made. Make 5 flowers.

Roll out rest of paste into a strip $\frac{1}{2}$-inch × 6 inches; snip with scissors down one 6-inch side. Cut into 5 pieces and roll up each to make centre stamens of flower. Fix in centre of flowers with egg white and paint yellow with a little colouring. Make leaves by colouring almond paste green, roll out thinly and cut diamond shapes from the paste. Cut out irregular points with a $\frac{1}{4}$-inch cutter or top of ball point pen, lay each leaf over the handle of a wooden spoon to dry out. Roll a few red berries from red coloured paste.

Arrange and fix flowers and leaves together on a 4-inch circle of thick card covered with foil, securing with dabs of royal icing. Use spare royal icing and almond paste to support a red candle in the centre. Leave overnight to become firm. Use the spare holly leaves to decorate the sides of the cake, securing with dabs of icing. Lift candle decoration onto centre of top of cake.

## CHRISTMAS PARCEL CAKE

*Make up Fruit Cake Mixture No. 1 (see p. 120) in a square 8-inch tin.*

You need not use almond paste, but either trim cake flat or reverse. Make up 1½ lb. flat icing and use to coat cake in the usual way, making sure edges and corners are neat. Lift onto an 11-inch cake board. Using a fine writing pipe and glacé icing, pipe a maze design all over the cake. Allow to harden. Fix two lengths of ribbon to cross cake in centre, tuck under bottom edges and seal with dabs of icing. Top cake with a ribbon pom-pom to match (which can be obtained from any stationer) and a suitable Christmas greetings card.

McDougalls Cookery Service

**Nowell Christmas Cake: an unusual theme for decoration, easy to carry out**

## NOWELL CHRISTMAS CAKE

*Make up Fruit Cake Mixture No. 1 (see p. 120) in an 8-inch round tin.*

Cover top and sides with 1½ lb. almond paste, reserving small piece for decoration wrapped in foil to keep moist. Prepare 1½ lb. royal icing, position cake on 10-inch board with a dab of icing, cover top and smooth. Add more sugar to rest of icing so that it will pull into points. Cover the sides, use a table knife to roughen the icing to represent snow. Wipe edge of board clean. Colour rest of icing brown with a little coffee essence. Fix choir boys in position with dabs of icing on top of cake. With remaining icing, use fine writing tube to pipe five parallel lines and a few notes in front of the choir boys. Roll out remaining piece of almond paste thinly, cut out slightly curved plaque. Fix to cake with dabs of icing. With same tube, and same icing, pipe "NOWELL" in centre with scrolls either side and line-dot decorations underneath it.

**Miniature Christmas Cakes: each child or guest can have an individually decorated cake, to make a Yuletide party fun; they are quicker to bake than a big cake, too**

## MINIATURE CHRISTMAS CAKES

The mixture suggested is moist but not too rich for children, to whom these tiny cakes will certainly appeal.

*Make up Children's Christmas Cake Mixture (see p. 122). Bake in 6 3 × 1½-inch moulds for 1½–2 hours in a very moderate oven.*

Make up 1½ lb. almond paste, roll out thinly, cut circles 5 inches in diameter. Brush cakes with boiled sieved apricot jam and place a circle of almond paste on each. Mould paste smoothly around sides and top of each cake. Make up 1½ lb. royal icing, use to coat the cakes in the usual way. Each can be decorated differently. Here are some suggestions. Pull icing into snow peaks all over cakes with a knife blade, then top with a holly sprig, a tiny tree ornament, or candle in a holder. Smooth out space round sides of some and tie round narrow red ribbon in a bow. Or make an igloo, building up icing in centre and marking all round with a fork. Top with eskimo figure and smooth out a "doorway" with the back of a spoon.

## SNOWFLAKE CHRISTMAS CAKE
(Colour Plate No. 7)

*Make up Fruit Cake Mixture No. 2 (see p. 121), in an 8-inch round tin.*

Make up 1½ lb. almond paste, using almond paste recipe No. 3, and coat the cake in the usual way. Make up 1½ lb. royal icing, including 3 drops of glycerine. Reserve a little for decoration. Cover cake with the icing, smoothing sides with a ruler, and using blade of a knife to pull up the top into peaks. Swirl centre area to make base for decoration. Mount on a 10-inch board with a dab of icing, and with a large writing tube pipe swirled blobs of reserved icing to finish base of cake. Cover edge of board with green ribbon, securing with Sellotape. Cut "snowflakes" from gold paper doileys and press lightly in place round sides of cake above the blobs. Choose a well-shaped twig, paint with glue and dip in gold or silver glitter dust, cut out both large and small "snowflakes" from 2 doileys, stick back to back, gold sides outwards, and attach to branches while glue is still tacky. (If covering of twig is disturbed by this process, sprinkle with more glitter dust and shake when dry.) Press twig firmly into centre of cake.

NOTE: Both silver and gold paper doileys can be cut up to make very unusual and delicate looking decorations, the shapes being inspired by the patterns of the doileys themselves. If to be placed flat against the sides or top of the cake they can be used single, but if both sides of the decoration are to be seen, two must be glued together back to back. In any case, this makes the decorations firmer to handle and position correctly.

Colman's Fine Semolina

**Snowflake Christmas Cake:** this original style of decoration, which is entirely different from the traditional theme, would be equally lovely in silver

Plate 7

Above—Snowman Cake: is fun for the children. Even the hat is easy, a strip of card 8 × 3 inches fastens round the back of his head, top of hat is a small circle cut from larger one which then forms the brim of his hat

Modern Woman

Right—Christmas Star Cake: has sides marked with a serrated icing scraper. Make an 8-star template from greaseproof paper to use as a guide for pricking out the star design on the cake surface

British Sugar Corporation

Plate 8

Modern Woman

**Top—German Christmas Cake: has no icing, but a beautifully glazed almond paste crown opening out to reveal glistening glacé cherries. Below— Christmas Chalet Cake: chocolate and raisin tiles for a fairytale house**

Plate 9

Kraft Foods

**Christmas Tree Cake:** an effective yet simple cake, made from Sponge Mixture baked in 2 swiss-roll tins. The cakes are cut to shape and sandwiched together, then iced with Philly icing and decorated with festive candles

Plate 10

## CHRISTMAS STAR CAKE

(Colour Plate No. 8)

*Make up Fruit Cake Mixture No. 1 (see p. 120) in an 8-inch round tin.*

Make up 1½ lb. almond paste and use to cover the cake in the usual way. Make up royal icing using 1½ lb. sieved icing sugar.

Coat the sides of the cake with a fairly thick layer of icing, using a palette knife to work the icing. (To make it easier, place the cake and board on a turntable, if available.) Take a serrated scraper and use to make the ridges on the sides of the cake—hold the scraper in your right hand at right angles to the side of the cake, and at the back. With your left hand rotate the turntable without moving the scraper, but keeping it lightly pressed against the surface of the icing, until the grooves meet. Leave to dry before flat icing the top.

Make an 8-inch template, from grease-proof paper, the diameter of the cake. Using the template as a guide, prick the star design with a pin on to the dry, flat-iced surface of the cake. Pipe lines using a No. 1 writing tube to continue the star shape. Pipe the outline of the star with dots using a No. 2 writing tube. Around the top and bottom edges of the cake, pipe rosettes with a No. 8 star tube.

From a small piece of almond paste coloured green make three holly leaves; from a small piece coloured red make tiny berries. Place in the centre. If liked sprinkle leaves with sieved icing sugar and top with a small glass bauble.

## SNOW SLIDE CAKE

*Make up Christmas Cake Mixture (see p. 119) in an 8-inch round tin.*

Make up 1 lb. almond paste and cover the top and sides of the cake in the usual way. Make up a first coat of royal icing with half an egg white, 5½ oz. sieved icing sugar and a few drops of lemon juice. Cover cake and allow to dry for 24 hours. Place on a board, then make up 1 lb. royal icing, of fairly stiff consistency to give body to the snow peaks. Cover the cake, lift icing into peaks with the blade of a knife. While icing is still soft scoop out depressions for the decorations. Smooth a snow slide for a toboggan and surround with miniature Christmas trees.

## CHRISTMAS TREE CAKE

(Colour Plate No. 10)

*Make up 2 batches of Sponge Mixture No. 2 (see p. 124) and bake in 2 swiss-roll tins.*

Make up filling and topping by creaming 1 3-oz. packet of Philadelphia Cream Cheese, then gradually work in 14 oz. sieved icing sugar and 3-4 tablespoons lemon juice.

Cut each cake into a Christmas tree shape, using a template cut from a piece of paper as a guide. Sandwich the two shapes together with a little of the icing. Colour 3 tablespoons of the remaining icing with a few drops of green food colouring. Spread the remainder of the white icing over the top of the cake and mark with a fork. Pipe a shell border (using a No. 7 star tube) around the edge of the "tree" with the green icing. Insert a candle at the end of each "branch" and surround the base with silver balls. Pipe "Xmas" with a No. 1 writing tube and green icing down the centre of the cake.

If liked the Victoria sponge mixture may be flavoured with a little grated orange rind. The trimmings from the two cakes can be used in a trifle, or for making chocolate truffles.

## GERMAN CHRISTMAS CAKE
(Colour Plate No. 9)

*Make up Fruit Cake Mixture No. 1 (see p. 120) in a 9-inch round tin.*

Make up 1 lb. almond paste. Brush over top of cake with sieved apricot jam. Take one-third almond paste and work into thin rope to fit round top edge of cake, press in place. Roll out remainder to round shape, cut to fit top of cake, press in place. Mark centre, make three 4-inch slashes crossing at centre to make six equal petals. Turn back petals, brush top of cake with egg wash. Bake in hot oven for a few minutes to glaze. Fill centre with glacé cherries. When cold tie red ribbon round sides of cake.

## CHRISTMAS CHALET CAKE
(Colour Plate No. 9)

*Make up Rich Chocolate Cake Mixture (see p. 126). Bake in a 2 lb. loaf tin in a moderate oven for 1¼ hours.*

Make up 1¼ lb. chocolate butter cream. Cover 8 oz. California seedless raisins with water, allow to stand for 5 minutes, drain and dry, chop half of them. Divide the cake in three equal layers. Reserve top layer. Put the two bottom layers together with a layer of butter cream, sprinkled with half the chopped raisins. Coat the top and sides with butter cream and press the whole raisins against the sides and dust them well with icing sugar. Sprinkle the remaining chopped raisins on top. Take the top layer of the cake and cut a strip 1 inch wide off the long side. Stand the remaining piece on end and cut down through the cake diagonally from corner to corner. Lay the wedges on top of the cake to form a sloping roof. Place on a square 10-inch board with a dab of butter cream. Pipe on the remaining butter cream with a No. 12 tube in rows of parallel shells to represent tiles. Cut a piece off the spare strip of cake to form the chimney. Dust the house and edge of board well with icing sugar. Decorate with trees and a

Father Christmas ornament, fixing them in place with dabs of icing. To make the Chalet as realistic as possible, try to keep the size of the ornaments in correct proportion to it.

## STAR-SPANGLED CHRISTMAS CAKE

*Make up Fruit Cake Mixture No. 2 (see p. 121) in an 8-inch round tin.*

Make up 1 lb. almond paste. Use this to coat cake in the usual way. Make up 1½ lb. royal icing, position cake on a 10-inch board with a dab of icing and then apply a fairly thin first coat. Cover remainder of icing with damp cloth while this dries, then coat cake again, smoothing top with palette knife. Add a little more icing sugar to rest of icing and coat sides and 1-inch border of top of cake, forming peaks with a table knife. Take icing out to edge of board. When dry, decorate top with tiny holly sprigs and silver paper stars.

Right—Star-spangled Christmas Cake: it's an easy one for beginners to make because instead of piped decorations you have only to arrange a constellation of silver paper stars and little holly sprigs on the top

Blue Band Bureau

Lower Left—Snowman Cake: it's also shown on Colour Plate 8, so you can see how to use natural, red and brown almond paste to fashion the details which make this cake so realistic it really does look like a miniature Snowman

Modern Woman

## SNOWMAN CAKE
(Colour Plate No. 8)

*Make up Rich Plain Cake Mixture (see p. 125) in the following way. Prepare a 1½ pt. pudding basin and a 7-inch flan tin with sloping sides. Put half the mixture into each, reserving enough to fill two paper cupcake cases for the head. Bake in the usual way, taking out cupcakes when done.*

Remove paper cases from cupcakes, and invert one on top of the other. Sandwich together with a little butter cream. Make up 1 lb. almond paste. Trim the other cakes flat, invert domed cake onto shallow cake, and sandwich with butter cream. Reserve about an ounce of almond paste for the decorations, and use rest to coat the head and body of the Snowman. Join together with butter cream. Make up 1 lb. royal icing. Stand the cake on a round 9-inch board,

smooth the icing over it with a palette knife, and spread a little icing round the base of the cake to represent snow. Bind tiny twigs round a larger one with raffia to make the broom. Press with a knob of almond paste against the side of the body before icing sets, secure with a wooden stick and ice over it. Colour some of the remaining almond paste red and some brown. Use to make the eyes, nose and buttons, and a thin rope of brown almond paste to outline fingers of hand. (First remove wooden stick when hand is firmly attached.) Make the cardboard top-hat from thin card painted black or from a discarded chocolate box. You need three pieces of card; a circle for the crown, strip to be joined for sides, a ring for the brim. Make the scarf from an inch-wide strip of red material fringed with wool.

## SQUARE CHRISTMAS CAKE

*Make up Fruit Cake Mixture No. 1 (see p. 120) in an 8-inch square tin, quantities as for a 7-inch round tin.*

Make 1½ lb. almond paste and use to coat the cake in the usual way. Make 1½ lb. royal icing, reserve a little for decoration. Ice top and sides of cake in the usual way, smooth corners with knife blade and shave off a groove along top edge for the piping. Mount cake on a 10-inch board with a dab of icing.

Cut out a 5-inch circle in stiff paper, put in centre of cake and prick round it with a clean pin. Using a No. 2 writing pipe, fill in the round with trellis. Colour a little of the remaining icing pale green and add icing sugar until it will pull up into points. Outline the centre circle with stars, using a small star pipe. Add a little more green colouring to the icing. Outline the holly leaves on top of cake with a medium writing pipe, then fill them in with more green icing, marking centre veins with a cocktail stick. Reserve remainder of this icing for the moment.

Stiffen some of the white icing until it will pull up into points. Using the same fine star tube as before, pipe along the top edge of the cake drawing the tube up and twisting the icing every ½-inch. Repeat this decoration along the edges of the cake just below the first line. Alternate the twists so they come in between those on top of the cake. Repeat this pattern twice down the corners of the cake.

Using the green icing, outline a triangle for the tops of the trees, placing these centrally one on each side. Fill in the triangles in green to resemble branches. Pipe a double line down from the branches for the stem.

Colour a tablespoonful of the remaining icing bright red, put three dots for holly berries near the leaves in each corner. Outline and fill in the pots for the trees, also in red. Pipe a shell pattern with a finely serrated star tube where the cake meets the board. Allow to dry. Arrange a group of sugar flowers and leaves with a dab of icing in the centre of the cake.

**Left—Square Christmas Cake:** you have a choice of making piped sugar or moulded flowers to fill the centre circle, or the space could be filled by piping in the words "A Merry Christmas" in red icing.

McDougalls Cookery Service

**Opposite—Book of Carols Cake:** if you enjoy fine piping with a writing tube you will want to try your hand at this neat reproduction of an open music book; practise the piping first on the paper template before you attempt it on the cake.

## BOOK OF CAROLS CAKE

*Make up Fruit Cake Mixture No. 1 (see p. 120) in rectangular tin 12 × 8 × 3½ inches deep, quantities as for 8-inch round tin, for 40 minutes at 350°F. (gas mark 4), then 1¾–2 hours at 275°F. (gas mark 1).*

Make 1½ lb. almond paste. Roll out just under half the paste on sugared paper to approximately 12 × 8 inches, brush over with beaten egg, place cake flat on paste, press well, neaten edges. Roll out 4 strips for sides from remaining almond paste, brush with beaten egg, press in position, trim and make joins neat. Reverse and allow to dry. To improvise a large enough cake board, cut one from a thick cardboard dress-box lid, 10 × 16 inches, cover with red crêpe paper or kitchen foil. Position cake centrally on this.

Make 1½ lb. royal icing. Ice top of cake, spread level with a ruler. Spread icing on sides of cake, finish with a serrated scraper or wide-toothed comb, to represent pages of a book. Wipe edges of board clean. Colour most of the remainder of the icing brown. Using a fine writing pipe, pipe the heading "THE HOLLY AND THE IVY" on the top of the right hand part of cake. Using a fine writing tube, put in the score of the first lines of the carol under the heading. On the left hand side pipe "CHRISTMAS CAROLS". Colour remaining icing green and decorate the border with holly berries and ivy leaves. Place a piece of red ribbon across centre of cake, tucking one end under and fixing with a dab of icing. Cut free end at an angle to represent book mark.

Cadbury Typhoo Food Advisory Service

**Star-time Christmas Cake: the star motif used on this cake makes a change
from the holly or snow scene decorations which are a traditional choice**

## STAR-TIME CHRISTMAS CAKE

*Make up Fruit Cake Mixture No. 1 (see p. 120) in
a round 8-inch tin.*

Make 1½ lb. almond paste and coat the
cake in the usual way. Make 1½ lb. flat icing
and use to coat cake evenly. When dry, make
up 1 lb. more flat icing, use a dab to position
cake on a 10-inch cake board, spread icing
around the edge of the board to join it to
the cake. To make a pattern for the star,
draw two concentric circles, 4 inches and 1½
inches in diameter on thin card. Mark 5
points equidistant round outer circle, and 5
points equidistant round inner circle, falling
between outer points. Join up with ruled
lines, then cut out. Place on top of the cake,
matching centre of star to centre of cake, and
prick round the edges with a pin. Using a

No. 2 writing tube, ice over the pricks to
show the star outline clearly. Use the same
tube and pipe parallel straight lines across
¼-inch apart until the whole of the inside
area is covered. Pipe at right angles to form
trellis pattern.

Using No. 6 star tube, pipe stars round the
edge of the star shape. Top every other one
with a silver ball. Using No. 15 star piping
tube, pipe shell edging around the top and
bottom edges. Repeat the shell edging slightly
smaller round the edge of the board. Place
tiny holly sprigs in the spaces between the
points of the star. Tie a red ribbon round the
sides of the cake in a bow.

Keep the star pattern with any others you
have made, as you may need to use them
again.

# Wedding and other Special Occasion Cakes

MAKING your own (or your daughter's) wedding cake is a most rewarding and really exciting project. If you don't feel able to build up an elaborate edifice on pillars, try this cake design which was planned for a busy woman to do quickly and easily.

## 3-TIER GARLAND WEDDING CAKE

*Make up Fruit Cake Mixture No. 2 (see p. 121) doubling quantities for 8-inch round tin, and dividing between 7-inch, 8-inch and 9-inch round tins.*

Make up sufficient almond paste to coat the top and sides of the three cakes (about 4-4½ lbs.). Coat with almond paste and store several days before icing. You will require 6 lb. icing sugar, 10 egg whites, a few drops of acetic acid and sufficient lemon juice to give a good coating consistency. This will be enough to coat cakes twice and for decorations.

Make paper templates of sides of all 3 cakes, divide each into 12 sections. Trace off design which repeats 3 loops and 1 triangle 3 times, making smaller as sections grow narrower for smaller cakes. Prick out pattern with a pin. Mount the bottom tier on a thick silver 10-inch board, middle tier and top tier on 9-inch and 8-inch thin silver boards respectively, using dabs of icing. Using star tube No. 21 pipe large rosettes round bases of cakes, then pipe round sides repeating loops lined with rosettes, and triangle pattern. Using star tube No. 8 fill in smaller rosettes as shown in photograph, dab icing

on backs of decorations and press in place. Use single silver leaves for top tiers, double leaves for bottom tier. Mount smaller cakes on to large cake, masking joins with more rows of rosettes. Place centre decoration on top, pipe double row of rosettes round base.

**3-tier Garland Wedding Cake: just one afternoon's work to mount and decorate**

## SILVER LEAF 3-TIER WEDDING CAKE

*Make up Fruit Cake Mixture No. 2 (see p. 121) dividing among 6-inch, 8-inch and 11-inch round tins.*

Make up sufficient almond paste to coat the top and sides of the three cakes (about 4½ lbs.). Coat with almond paste and store for several days before icing. You will require 6 lb. icing sugar, 10 egg whites, 1 teaspoonful lemon juice and 4 teaspoonfuls of glycerine to coat all three cakes twice. This should leave sufficient icing for the decorations. Position all three of the cakes with a dab of icing on 9-inch, 11-inch and 14-inch boards respectively.

Ice the tops and then the sides of the cakes, taking out to edge of board, allowing the top coat of icing to dry before the sides are iced. To obtain a flat smooth surface, allow the first coat to dry thoroughly before giving the cake a second coat. Leave to dry thoroughly before decorating. For this and mounting the cakes, you will require 6 3½-inch round white pillars, 24 silver leaves and a small silver vase of fresh flowers or a white sugar ornament.

Make a paper template for the tops of all three cakes, divide larger cakes into 8 sections, and small cake into 4 sections, marking with a pin. For the 11-inch cake also mark on an inner circle of 4-inch radius 3 equidistant points (for the pillars) and for the 8-inch cake, the same on a circle of 3-inch radius. Remove template and mark these points with dots of icing. Use a star tube No. 8 to make the top outside border with an inverted "e" pattern, going from small to large, to small again. This process is repeated 8 times around the 2 larger cakes, 4 times around the small cake. Using a No. 2 writing tube, pipe loops joining the points of these decorations on top of the cakes, and groups of 4 smaller swagged loops, festooning the sides between the same points. Using the same tube, pipe a maze design all over the edge of the cake boards and finish edges with dots. With a No. 22 ribbon tube, pipe a ribbon border, doubling every inch, against the sides of the cakes. Fix the silver leaves in place before the icing is quite dry, using four groups of 2 leaves and 4 of single leaves on the bottom tier, two groups of 2 leaves only on the middle tier, 4 single leaves only on the top tier. Place 3 pillars in marked position on bottom tier, mount middle tier, place pillars and mount top tier. Add vase or decoration.

**Silver Leaf 3-tier Wedding Cake: round cakes repeat a classic design which is simple and elegant as it stands, could be elaborated by adding motifs to the sides**

Blue Band Bureau

Silver Horseshoe 3-tier Wedding Cake: beautifully balanced design of squares and triangles which are automatically proportioned to the different sized cakes

## SILVER HORSESHOE 3-TIER WEDDING CAKE

*Make up Fruit Cake Mixture No. 2 (see p. 121), dividing among 5-inch, 7-inch and 10-inch square tins.*

Make up sufficient almond paste to coat the tops and sides of the three cakes (allow about 5½ lbs.). Coat with almond paste and store several days before icing. Prepare the royal icing, as for the cake on the opposite page. Position the cakes with a dab of icing on 3 square boards, 8-inch, 10-inch and 14-inch respectively, first edging boards with silver paper decoration.

Ice as suggested for the cake on the opposite page. For mounting the cakes you will require 8 3½-inch square pillars, 12 silver horseshoe ornaments, and a small silver vase of fresh flowers or alternatively a white sugar ornament.

Make a paper template for the tops of all three cakes, mark centres of the four sides on each cake and draw in a square from these points on the templates. Mark these squares in with a pin. Also mark centre of each side of the squares on the two larger cakes, as points on which to position the pillars. Remove templates and using fine writing tube No. 1, outline the inner squares with dots. Using the same tube pipe rows of parallel lines to each row of dots out towards the corner, then fill in the trellis with rows of parallel lines at right angles, using line from corner to centre point where pillar will touch as guide. Using star tube No. 8, pipe small stars all round edges of tops of the three cakes, and overpipe the dots which outline the squares with small stars. Using fine writing tube No. 1 pipe a maze design out to the edges of the boards. With writing tube No. 2, pipe a reversed "e" pattern round the side

edges of the tops of the cakes, and a larger reversed "e" pattern against the sides of the bases of the cakes.

While icing is still not quite set, press silver paper horseshoes against the 4 corners of all the cakes. Place 4 pillars in position on bottom tier, mount middle tier; place 4 more pillars in position, mount top tier, and put decoration on top.

When assembling the cake, make sure that the corners of each tier fall exactly above those of the tier underneath, to keep it symmetrical.

**Medallion Wedding Cake:** Use round pastry cutters and boat-shaped patty tins as a guide for the design, pricking round with a pin or pressing lightly against icing

**Top Left—**No. 2 writing tube is used to make fine trellis over boat-shaped tins greased with lard. Warm under side of tin to remove and make more than are required to allow for breakage when removing baskets from tins

**Bottom Left—**Sit with cake raised on books under turn-table while icing decorations on sides so that wrist is not bent at awkward angle. Trace monogram on template and prick out on side

Modern Woman

## MEDALLION WEDDING CAKE

*Make up Fruit Cake Mixture No. 2 (see p. 121), dividing between a 6-inch and a 10-inch round tin.*

Coat with almond paste (about 3 lbs.) and store for 2-4 days before icing. You will require 3 lb. icing sugar, 6 egg whites, ½ teaspoon lemon juice and 2 teaspoonfuls glycerine to coat both cakes twice, and decorate.

Position both cakes on 7-inch and 11-inch boards respectively. Coat twice and dry well. Make paper templates for sides of both cakes and top of lower tier, dividing sides into 9 sections, top of lower tier into 3 sections. With No. 29 ribbon tube pipe dividers down sides between sections. Prick round 2½-inch cutter held against sides in the centre of each section for lower tier, 1½-inch cutter for top tier. With No. 6 star tube pipe rosettes round all these circles.

With same tube, on top tier pipe festoons of 5 rosettes each above each circle, and make a border of rosettes round bases of both cakes. Finish top tier with rosettes above each divider and a line edging using No. 2 writing tube.

On top of lower tier arrange 3 boat-shape patty tins equidistant with outer points centred on monograms. Prick round. Place lattice baskets on these outlines, pipe rosettes round base of each. Between them position three round pillars with dabs of icing, pipe two rows of rosettes round each, fix horseshoe ornament in centre of cake. Press six heather sprays, 2 either side of each basket, in place before icing sets. Finish top edge with rosettes and line edging. To finish sides of lower tier, fill in circles in groups of 3. No. 1, trellis using No. 2 writing tube; No. 2, entwined monogram of bride and groom pricked out through side template, with same tube; No. 3, horseshoe stuck in place with a dab of icing.

Place top tier in position on the pillars and put the sugar horseshoe ornament on top of the cake.

## SPRINGTIME BIRTHDAY CAKE

*Make up Fruit Cake Mixture No. 1 (see p. 120) in
an 8-inch round tin.*

Coat with almond paste and store for
several days before icing. For pale yellow flat
icing you will require 1 lb. icing sugar, 2 egg
whites and yellow colouring.

Stand the cake on its upturned tin. Pile
icing into centre of cake, use a palette knife
to spread evenly over top and remove excess
from the sides. Use an icing ruler to form a
flat top and remove any surplus from edges.
Spread remaining icing around the sides, reserving a little for edge of board, and smooth
with a palette knife. Trim the bottom edge
and allow to dry. Position the cake on a 10-
inch board with a dab of icing and spread a
little icing around the edge.

Make up a further 1 lb. flat icing for the
decoration. Using a No. 2 writing tube decorate edge with inch-long loops, alternately
plain and formed of dots, as shown in photograph. Using a No. 8 star tube pipe shell
round the top and bottom edges of the cake.
Finish edge of board in the same way. Decorate top of cake with spring flowers made
from royal icing.

Using No. 1 writing tube, trace outlines of
the chosen flowers from a suitable post card
or birthday card, onto waxed paper. (In this
design we have primroses, harebells and narcissi.) It is advisable to "anchor" the piece
of paper and move card underneath it. When
outlines have set "run in" the thin royal icing
using greaseproof paper icing bag with small
hole cut in the end. Allow flowers to dry
overnight and then using clean paint brush
and edible colouring, paint with suitable
colours. The narcissi are piped, using a No.
11 petal tube. Fix flowers on the cake with a
little royal icing.

Colour a little more icing pale green and
pipe suitable leaves directly onto the cake
with a No. 2 writing tube for narcissi leaves,
and a greaseproof paper bag with the top

**Springtime Birthday Cake: features a
decoration of piped and run-in group of
spring flowers**

cut to a sharp inverted "V" or arrowhead
for the primrose leaves. Make holes for
candles in the cake with a skewer and sharpen
ends of candles before sticking into cake.
Fix narrow band of green ribbon round
sides of cake.

**Top right**—Pipe out the
narcissi shapes in white
royal icing as shown in
photographs on p. 30, let
dry out for 2 or 3 days,
then paint in "trumpet"
centres with yellow food
colouring and paint brush

**Bottom right**—Use No. 2
writing tube and icing
tinted pale green to pipe
outlines of long narcissi
leaves and single lines
for stems, placing 5 of
the prepared heads in the
icing before it dries.
Using No. 42 petal tube,
pipe more leaves at base

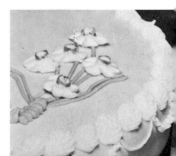

Cadbury Typhoo Food
Advisory Service

## SWEETHEARTS WEDDING CAKE

(Colour Plate No. 1)

*Make up Fruit Cake Mixture No. 2 (see p. 121), and divide between 6-inch and 11-inch square tins.*

Coat both cakes with almond paste and store for several days before icing. You will require 4 lb. icing sugar, 8 egg whites, 2 tea-spoonfuls glycerine and a few teaspoonfuls lemon juice. This will be sufficient for 2 coats of icing and the decoration. (You also need 4 3-inch square pillars, 16 tiny silver leaves, 16 larger leaves, 8 small horseshoes and 8 small pink sugar roses; 1 square 13-inch board and 1 square 7-inch board; pink ribbon decoration for top cake.)

Have ready 2 dozen flooded pink heart plaques, 4 large, 12 medium and 8 small. Make a few extra in case of breakages. Make a template of the design for the tops of both cakes, marking the centre of each side as a guide to position central heart directly under it. Mark off a triangle at each corner 4½ inches across the long side, using a No. 1 writing tube. Fill in with straight parallel lines right to corners. On sides of larger cake, place the heart plaques (1 large and 2 medium) in position on each side, with a dab of soft icing, and using same writing tube,

outline with tiny white dots. Outline the edge of the triangles on top of the cake with the same dots. With a No. 6 star tube outline the top edge of the cake with a double row of small stars and the bottom edge with 2 rows of shell piping, using the same star tube.

Mount pairs of small silver leaves at the top and larger leaves at the bottom corners, centred with a sugar rose. Arrange the 4 pillars evenly in place to hold the top tier, and affix with a dab of icing. Mount a horse-shoe at the base of each pillar. Repeat the decorations on top tier in the same way, omit-ting the pillars and adding the required central decoration and a horseshoe half-way along the top edge of each side.

## PINK RIBBON BIRTHDAY CAKE

(Colour Plate No. 12)

*Make up Fruit Cake Mixture No. 1 (see p. 120) in an 8-inch round tin.*

Coat with almond paste and with royal icing in the usual way, reserving ½ lb. icing for the decorations. Position cake with a dab of icing on an 11-inch board. Make a tem-plate for top of cake, marking 2 parallel lines each ½-inch away from centre. Prick out with pin. Leaving this inch-wide band free, pipe over the 2 lines with a No. 1 writing tube and cover top of cake with trellis diag-onally to these lines. With a No. 6 star tube pipe stars round top and bottom edges

**Sweethearts Wedding Cake: the pink sugar hearts are iced in outline and flooded with glacé icing to add a charming and romantic touch to the sides of the cake**

Draw hearts of various sizes on stiff paper, cover with larger sheets of waxed paper marked off into squares. Trace out-line of heart with glacé icing and fine writing tube and at once fill in with softer icing. Move waxed paper across and repeat

Roederer Rich Champagne

60

Trellis Wedding Cake: for a small party this would be an excellent size to choose, and the decorations could be delicately tinted to match the flowers

McDougalls Cookery Service

against side of cake. Tint rest of icing pink, pipe another row of stars inside white stars and a few stars either side of the words "HAPPY BIRTHDAY" (piped with No. 1 writing tube). Fix wide pink ribbon round sides of cake.

## TRELLIS WEDDING CAKE

*Make up Fruit Cake Mixture No. 1 (see p. 120) in an 11-inch round tin.*

Coat with almond paste and royal icing in the usual way, reserving ½ lb. icing for the decorations. Divide the cake into 5 around the top edge. Using a tea-plate mark 5 half-circles, each one joining 2 adjacent marked points. Position cake with a dab of icing on a 12-inch board. Using a No. 1 writing tube,

pipe parallel lines across the half-circles, and again at right angles. Outline this trellis pattern with small stars, using star tube No. 8. With a skewer, mark out 5 straight lines, running from each marked point on top of the cake diagonally across the side to finish on the cake board at the centre of the next half-circle. Pipe a row of stars along these lines. With the same star tube pipe an edging around the top and bottom edges of the cake, looping every inch. Finish side diagonals with a silver leaf ornament fixed with a dab of icing beneath the top star of each diagonal, and a silver horseshoe ornament fixed above the bottom star of each diagonal. As a contrast to the more conventional type of sugar ornament, place a tiny vase of freesias or lilies of the valley on top of the cake.

Cadbury Typhoo Food Advisory Service

**Basket-trimmed Wedding Cake: make the lattice baskets on special icing nails and have a few extras in reserve since they are very fragile to handle and mount**

## BASKET-TRIMMED WEDDING CAKE

*Make up Fruit Cake Mixture No. 1 (see p. 120), dividing between 6-inch and 10-inch round tins.*

Coat with almond paste and store for several days before icing with flat icing. You will require 3 lb. icing sugar, 6 egg whites and 3 teaspoonfuls glycerine to coat both cakes, and for raised trellis work. Lightly grease pyramid shaped icing nails. With a No. 2 writing tube pipe the trellis onto the nails (2 shapes on each nail). Allow to dry for 2-3 days. Warm slightly to soften the grease and remove carefully. For the illustrated decoration 28 half-pyramid shapes are required, but you should make one or two more in case of breakage. Make the shapes for the top tier slightly smaller.

Position the cakes on 8-inch and 12-inch boards respectively with dabs of icing. Make up 1 lb. flat icing for decorating. Spread icing round the edge of each board to join it to the cake and form a border. Using a paper template, divide top and sides of each cake into 8 sections, prick out the positions for the baskets, mark positions for 4 pillars. Arrange baskets as illustrated alternately round the top and sides of each cake, 2 to each section, sticking in place with a little icing. Using No. 6 star tube pipe stars round the edges of the trellis work. Using a No. 15 star tube, make a shell edging round the top and bottom edges against the sides of both cakes and also at the edge of both boards. Repeat this round the top edge of both cakes. Make 38 small white sugar roses (either piped with a small rose tube, or moulded from satin icing tinted very pale pink). Place groups of 3 roses and tiny silver leaves on the sides of both cakes with dabs of icing, between the baskets. Position pillars with dabs of icing, place top tier on firmly and add bell ornament.

## THREE CANDLE BIRTHDAY CAKE

*Make up Fruit Cake Mixture No. 2 (see p. 121) in an 8-inch round tin.*

Coat with almond paste in the usual way and store several days before icing. You will require 1 lb. icing sugar, 2 egg whites, a few drops lemon juice and a small teaspoonful glycerine to coat the cake twice and decorate. Mount the cake first on a 10-inch board with a dab of icing, and coat twice, taking second coat out to edge of board. Tint rest of icing pale pastel shade. Using a paper template divide top of cake into 8 sections; with a pin mark centre and 8 points on edge with a dot of icing. With a No. 6 star tube pipe a border round the top edge, making an inverted "e" pattern going from small to large, to small again. This process is repeated 8 times round the cake until border is covered. With the same tube pipe round the base of cake in an upright "e" pattern, slightly spacing out the loops. With a No. 1 writing tube, pipe a delicate garland inside each scroll in each of the 8 sections on top of the cake, alternate lines broken with dots, and lines broken with dots and a 5-petal flower. With the same tube, write "HAPPY BIRTHDAY", so that top of first "p" in "Happy" covers centre dot on icing. Place candle holders behind this and fix narrow ribbon to match pastel icing round cake.

## LUCKY HORSESHOE 21st BIRTHDAY CAKE

*Make up Fruit Cake Mixture No. 1 (see p. 120), quantities as for 8-inch round cake in a greased and lined horseshoe tin 9¾ × 9¾ inches placed on an upturned baking sheet, lined with double grease-proof paper to act as a base.*

Remove tin and paper from cake, wrap and store very carefully to avoid cracking until required. Coat with almond paste, cutting out round cake inverted onto paste for top, and covering sides and ends as for a square cake while still inverted. Turn right way up, place cake on 3 small cake tins so that the inside of the horseshoe is free and not resting on the supports. Leave several days before icing. You will require 1½ lb. icing sugar and 4 egg whites for flat icing to cover and decorate.

Again, place the cake on 3 cake tins so that the inside of the horseshoe is free and not resting on the supports. Cover with icing, smooth with a table knife from the outside to the centre and from the centre to the outside clockwise. Carefully transfer cake to a turn-table or large upturned cake tin. Cover outside with icing, then 2 blunt ends, allow to dry. Cover top of cake, smoothing with an icing ruler. Allow to dry. Stiffen remaining icing slightly and colour it pale blue or pink. Mark round outer edge of horseshoe every ½-inch. Position cake on an 11-inch

Stork Cookery Service

Above—Three Candle Birthday Cake: the floral style of decoration is delicate and feminine, and would appeal to older girls as much as to a three-year-old

Below—Lucky Horseshoe 21st Birthday Cake: if you can buy or borrow a horseshoe tin, this original birthday cake is equally suitable for any other occasion when you wish the recipient good luck

McDougalls Cookery Service

board with a dab of icing, place board on turn-table or upturned tin. Turn cake so that open ends of horseshoe are to the left. Starting with the side of cake furthest away from you, pipe lines of icing with a No. 1 writing tube, using the ½-inch marks as a guide and keeping the icing parallel with the end of the horseshoe. Carry on up to the top rounded end. Repeat this process with the side near you. As the blunt ends of the cake are at an angle the icing lines will cross where the horseshoe bends round. Starting from the centre of the cake and working outwards pipe diagonal lines, beginning on top of the original trellis and finishing in between as shown in photograph.

Still using the writing tube decorate the 4 edges of the cake with 3 zig-zag lines. Space out 21 candles as shown in photograph and pipe round bases with a No. 8 star tube. Using same tube pipe stars round inside and outside of cake where it meets the board and round the blunt ends of horseshoe.

Top left—Pipe the stars round top edge of cake, 7 to every section; then a ring of 4 stars to each section, centred on the first 7; then 3 stars in each section being careful last star falls on marked point on inner circle for even spacing

Bottom left—Use a writing tube to pipe in the greeting over the letters already pricked out through template with a pin to give a professional finish to the cake

Coffee Information Bureau

## COFFEE ENGAGEMENT CAKE
(Colour Plate No. 11)

This is a most unusual celebration cake which could be used for a wedding anniversary or, with different wording on the top, for an examination success.

*Make up a coffee sponge cake (see p. 124) in an 8-inch deep round tin.*

You will also need 6 oz. coffee butter cream for the filling, 12 oz. white glacé icing to cover the cake, and 4 oz. coffee glacé icing for the decorations, the recipes for which will all be found in the appropriate sections.

Cut the cake in half and spread with butter cream. Sandwich together again. Make up the white glacé icing, pour onto the top of the cake and spread very carefully over top and sides, to coat smoothly. Place cake on a wire tray over a plate to catch icing drips. Make up the coffee glacé icing to a stiff consistency.

Using paper template divide top edge of cake into 8 sections, and mark out 8 points equidistant between the sections on a concentric circle of 2½-inch radius. Using the coffee glacé icing and a No. 8 star tube, pipe round edge of top of cake, making 7 large rosettes in each section. Fill in a second row of rosettes, centred on each basic row of 7, then 2 rosettes and finally 1 rosette at the point marked on the inner circle. Repeat in each section to form a central star pattern. Trim round bottom edge of cake neatly, transfer to a turn-table raised on a book if necessary so that sides can be iced at a comfortable height when seated. With a No. 3 writing tube, pipe in the names of the couple or other appropriate message.

Make a side template, write the word "CONGRATULATIONS" spaced out to fill half length, prick out round the sides of the cake. To make sure the letters are evenly spaced divide half the circumference of the cake into 15 equal parts, one for each letter. Ice the word in with the same writing tube.

Coffee Information Bureau

**Coffee Engagement Cake: a really striking looking cake which young people
may enjoy more than a fruit cake with traditional almond paste and icing**

Plate 11

Above—Pink Ribbon Birthday Cake: shows the most effective way to use a pastel colour with white for the decorations of a child's birthday cake

McDougalls Cookery Service

Left—Stork Christening Cake: roses moulded from pink Satin Icing Paste set off the effect of pale blue piping on a white cake. The piping could be in pale pink

Stork Cookery Service

Plate 12

Right—Raspberry Layer Cake: pale pink icing coats a simple teatime sponge, and raspberries moulded from tinted almond paste form part of the effective decoration

Davis Gelatine

Below—Oranges and Lemons Cake: an effective decoration can be made from a few crystallised orange and lemon slices

Cadbury Typhoo Food Advisory Service

Plate 13

**Gala 21st Birthday Cake:** for this wonderful occasion, make an impressive
cake and decorate it with an intricate pattern of strands and rosettes

Plate 14

# GALA 21st BIRTHDAY CAKE
(Colour Plate No. 14)

*Make up Fruit Cake Mixture No. 1 (see p. 120) in a 10-inch square tin.*

Coat the cake with almond paste in the usual way, store for a few days before coating with royal icing. You will require 2 lb. icing sugar, 4-5 egg whites and 1 teaspoonful lemon juice to coat the cake and for decorations. Position the cake on a 12-inch board with icing, spread top and sides smoothly, take icing out to the edges of the board. Allow to harden. Stiffen up the coating icing to a firm piping consistency and using a No. 21 star tube, pipe a border of large rosettes round top and bottom edges of the cake. To finish the top edge pipe smaller rosettes, using a No. 6 star tube, opposite the large ones, but 1½ inches in from the edge. Pipe a similar band of small rosettes around the sides of the cake 1½ inches below the top edge. Leave to dry. Thin down the icing a little and with a No. 1 writing tube pipe diagonal strands of icing from the large to the small stars in one direction, all round the cake. Leave to dry, then pipe diagonal strands in the opposite direction. This will give the effect of loops all around the cake.

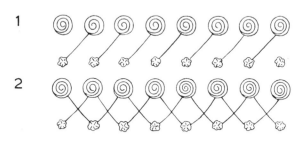

The writing may be done off the cake—it is much easier. Sketch out the lettering "HAPPY BIRTHDAY" on a sheet of white paper and cover with a piece of wax paper, placing both sheets on a baking tin or back of a tray so that paper is kept flat. Using a No. 3 writing tube and icing tinted apricot pink, pipe onto the wax paper, tracing out greeting on white paper underneath. Leave

48 hours to dry out then carefully remove and fix in position on the cake with icing, diagonally from corner to corner. The "21" is similarly piped out in outline onto wax paper with a No. 1 writing tube and the centre flooded with softer icing. Harden off and place in lower front corner. (Use same icing and No. 1 writing tube to fill edges of board with maze pattern.) Decorate remaining corner with a group of 3 large sugar-paste roses tinted to match apricot pink icing, and leaves tinted green. Fix a wide pink ribbon round the cake.

# CRADLE CHRISTENING CAKE

*Make up Fruit Cake Mixture No. 1 (see p. 120), multiplying quantities for 8-inch round cake by 1½, in a 9-inch square tin. Coat with almond paste and royal icing as for Square Christmas Cake.*

Make 12 sugar flowers, rosebuds for a girl, forget-me-nots for a boy. Make a template for top of cake, marking "s"-shaped scrolls in 3 corners and position for cradle ornament in fourth corner, and flowers. Affix flowers with icing.

Using a No. 6 star tube, finish top edge of cake and base where cake meets board with stars. Colour a little icing pale blue or pink, pipe the child's name, date, etc., diagonally across centre of the cake, using a No. 2 writing tube. Use same tube and icing to make small dots round the edge of the cake close to the stars. Arrange cradle decoration on corner of cake and fix wide pink or blue ribbon round the sides of the cake.

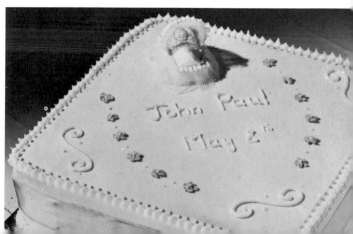

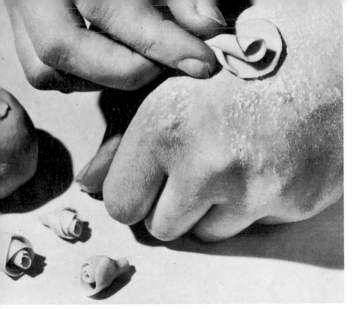

## STORK CHRISTENING CAKE
(Colour Plate No. 12)

*Make up Fruit Cake Mixture No. 2 (see p. 121) in an 8-inch round tin.*

Coat the cake with almond paste and royal icing in the usual way, giving 2 coats. Dry thoroughly. Make up some more royal icing, position cake on a 10-inch board and cover board smoothly to edge with icing.

Make up about $\frac{3}{4}$ lb. Satin Icing (see p. 22), tinted pink. Make up 23 roses, with a few extra to allow for breakages, as follows. To make the petals, place a piece of Satin Icing the size of a large mimosa ball on the back of the hand. Flatten out thinly to a smooth petal shape, with the forefinger of the other hand. Make 3 petals to form one "rose". After making the first petal, roll it round and round to form the centre of the rose. Then fold the other petals round the first, turning the tips slightly outwards. Leave to dry and carefully cut off the "stems", if too long.

Mark off top and base of cake into 8 even sections with small dots of icing. Using a No. 6 star tube, pipe a border round top outer edge of cake, following an inverted "e" pattern going from small to large, to small again. Repeat this process 8 times around the cake until the border is covered, and the same pattern round the base of the cake. With a No. 1 writing tube, pipe 8 loops around sides of cake attaching loops to the top border pattern. With the same tube, pipe small dots of icing over the piped loops. Position stork ornament with a dab of icing. Colour the remaining icing a pale blue and with a No. 1 writing tube pipe small dots round its base. Decorate top of cake with 5 groups of 3 roses, placed 1 inch in from the border, leaving space for child's name. Attach with dots of blue icing; using same tube pipe name in, and position 8 roses round the base of the cake with dots of icing on either side. Fix narrow blue ribbon round sides of cake.

Stork Cookery Service

# *Seasonal and Novelty Birthday Cakes*

I F you are baking for a birthday, for an Easter party, or some other special date on the calendar, it is most satisfying to be able to produce a cake that is appropriate to the day, and tastes every bit as good as it looks. This Rose Cake, for example, in the shape of our national emblem, would be a natural choice on many occasions.

## ENGLISH ROSE CAKE

*Make up Basic White Cake Mixture (see p. 123) in a 10-inch round tin.*

Make up a meringue, for which you will need 3 egg whites, a pinch of salt, 6 oz. castor sugar and 1 oz. cornflour. Whisk the egg whites with the pinch of salt until foamy, then gradually beat in half of the sugar and continue beating until the mixture stands in stiff peaks. Sift the rest of the sugar with the cornflour and fold gently into the mixture.

When the cake is cold, divide top into 5 sections and cut out a wide inverted "v" from each section, to form 5 "petals". Place the cake on a wooden board, cover thickly with the meringue, leaving a little for decoration. Using a No. 8 star tube pipe the remainder of the meringue all round the top edge, completing each petal separately and bringing it in towards the centre. Dry off for 1-1½ hours in a very cool oven.

When cake is dry and firm place on a large round silver board. Arrange a group of mimosa balls in the centre and cut fine slivers of angelica for stamens. Arrange these in groups of 2, centred in each petal. Cut 5 diamond-shaped leaves of angelica and push into sides of cake just under top edging where the petals join.

(NOTE: It is important not to overheat oven or meringue may discolour.)

English Rose Cake: you can learn how to cover a cake with a meringue which is baked on like an icing after the cake is decorated, if you study the method used here. Be careful not to spoil the coating by colouring it in the oven, which should be set at gas mark ¼ or electric 150°F.

Brown & Polson

Brown & Polson

## WITCHES HALLOWE'EN CAKE

*Make up Chocolate Sponge Mixture (see p. 126) increasing quantities by ½, in 2 10-inch tins.*

Make up a filling as follows:—Mix a packet pineapple flavoured cornflour and 4 oz. sugar smoothly with a little taken from ¼ pt. cold water, put the rest on to heat. Add mixed cornflour and allow to boil for 1 minute stirring constantly. Put in a basin, cover and leave to get cold, then beat thoroughly and beat in 4 oz. margarine. Remove top third from 5 small oranges, scoop out pulp, remove pith and chop pulp roughly. Blend with 12 maraschino cherries cut in quarters, ¼ lb. grapes seeded and quartered, and the pineapple cornflour mixture. Use to sandwich the cakes together, smoothing filling round edge. Make cuts in orange skins to represent eyes, nose and mouth. Make a hat for each from thin black card. Sieve a

little icing sugar over the top of cake and decorate with the oranges.

## BLACK CAT CAKE

*Make up Chocolate Sponge Mixture (see p. 126) in 2 7-inch sandwich tins.*

Make up 8 oz. butter cream, flavour with lemon essence and colour pale yellow with food colouring. Use about ⅓ to sandwich cakes together. Coat cake smoothly with rest of butter cream. Tint 2 oz. almond paste brown with food colouring, cut out tiny stars and crescent moons, and a cat shape (using a penny as guide for body, a half-penny for

head), tiny triangles for ears, and 2-inch narrow strip for tail. Roll tiny "berries" from another 2 oz. almond paste, tinted yellow. Arrange decorations as shown in photograph, using real glossy dark green leaves to decorate plate and centre of cake. (Cat-shape biscuits in background are baked from chocolate flavoured biscuit dough, coated with chocolate glacé icing, "faces" piped with white glacé icing.)

## PRIMROSE DAY CAKE

*Make up Whisked Sponge Mixture No. 1 (see p. 124) in 2 7-inch sandwich tins.*

Sandwich the 2 cakes together with raspberry jam. To make a chocolate flavoured icing, put 3 Milky Bars with 6 tablespoonfuls water in a basin, and melt over hot water. Stir in 1¾ lb. icing sugar and add sufficient yellow food colouring to tint primrose yellow. Put a third of the mixture on one side and cover. Stir in a further 6-8 oz. icing sugar to the remainder and a little more colouring, to give a good consistency for rolling out.

Roll out thinly and cut round tin as guide for circle to cover top of the cake. Using a small heart-shaped cutter, cut 15 "petals" and arrange on the cake in groups of 5 to make 3 "primroses", the points of the hearts placed all pointing in to the centre of each flower. Fasten in place with dabs of soft icing. Using a No. 6 star tube and soft icing, pipe lines between the petals and one star in the centre of each flower. Spread the rest of the soft icing round the sides of the cake and rough into points with a knife.

By tinting the icing pale pink instead of yellow, you could vary the flower decoration to make pink Alexandra Day roses.

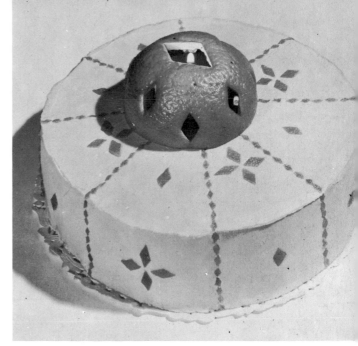

## ORANGE SURPRISE CAKE

*Make up Sponge Mixture No. 2 (see p. 124) in 2 7-inch sandwich tins.*

Cream together 3 oz. Family Margarine and 5 oz. sieved icing sugar. Gradually beat in enough orange food colouring to tint cream icing pale orange. Cut ⅓ off top of an orange. Scoop out all the flesh and pith without damaging shell, and make attractive diamond cut-outs with the point of a sharp knife in it. Remove all pith from the flesh, and chop. Mix with ⅓ of the cream icing and use to sandwich the cake together. Cover top and sides smoothly with rest of cream icing and mark off into 8 sections, radiating from centre of cake across top and down sides. Using peel from another orange, cut out a number of tiny diamonds and about 40 larger diamonds. Use to decorate the cake, pressing lightly into the icing.

Place a night-light exactly in centre of cake, light it and cover carefully with the prepared orange shell.

NOTE: Make sure there is a fairly large diamond just above the night-light so that the flame will not scorch the orange skin.

Valentine Ring Cake: the effect of putting small almond paste hearts of a different colour against the sides of the cake is very striking—they can also be tinted pale pink instead of green, if you prefer the effect, or merely strengthen the natural colour of the almond paste with saffron yellow

Cadbury Typhoo Food Advisory Service

## VALENTINE RING CAKE

*Make up Chocolate Sponge Mixture (see p. 126) in 2 7-inch sandwich tins.*

When cool use a plain cutter to cut a circle from the centre of one sponge about $1\frac{1}{2}$ inches in diameter.

Make up $\frac{1}{2}$ lb. almond paste, tint pale green with food colouring, and roll out $\frac{1}{4}$-inch thick. Cut out 16 heart shapes.

Make up 1 lb. plain butter cream, reserve 3 tablespoonfuls, and add 1 tablespoonful cocoa to the remaining butter cream. Spread the whole layer of sponge with chocolate butter cream and place the ring of sponge on top.

Spread the sides and top evenly with more chocolate butter cream. Put onto a cake board or serving plate. Mark off 8 sections on sides and top of cake. Arrange marzipan hearts against sides, and in spaces between them, round the top of the cake. Using a No. 6 star tube pipe stars of plain butter cream round top edge and between hearts on top of cake. With No. 8 star tube pipe shell border round the base and inner edge of cake, and finish with the same tube and chocolate butter cream in large rosettes round outer edge of board.

## VALENTINE HEART CAKE

*Make up Chocolate Victoria Sandwich Mixture (see p. 126) in 2 heart-shaped sandwich tins.*

Make up a butter cream as follows:—beat together 5 oz. butter and 10 oz. icing sugar. Add a little warm water to give a creamy consistency. Blend 1 tablespoonful Bournville cocoa with a little boiling water and allow to cool. Beat this into $\frac{1}{4}$ of the prepared butter cream. To the remaining $\frac{3}{4}$ add sufficient cochineal to give a pale pink colour.

Make a glacé icing with 6 oz. icing sugar, and colour pale pink.

Spread pink butter cream between the layers of the cake and cover the top with the pink glacé icing. Allow to set. Mount the cake on a round or heart-shaped board, large enough to show at least 1 inch border all round. Using No. 8 star tube and the remaining pink butter cream pipe stars around the base and to cover the filling. With the same tube pipe stars of chocolate butter cream round the top edge. With a No. 2 writing tube outline a smaller heart 1 inch in from the edge, and another smaller heart formed of dots inside this. (Cut out heart shape in card and prick round this with a pin for guide if necessary.)

## FIVE HEARTS CAKE

Make up the following cake mixture:—
Mix 5 tablespoonfuls corn oil, 5 tablespoonfuls water and the yolks of 2 eggs together. Sift together 5 oz. plain flour, 1 oz. cornflour, 4 oz. castor sugar, and $\frac{1}{2}$ level teaspoon salt, then add to the corn oil mixture. Beat well to form a smooth, slack batter. Add the grated rind of $\frac{1}{2}$ orange and 1 dessertspoonful Cointreau. Beat the whites of the eggs till foamy, add another 2 oz. castor sugar and beat until the mixture holds in peaks, then fold lightly into the batter. Turn into a greased 9 or 10-inch round cake tin and bake for 45-50 minutes in a moderate oven. Turn out and leave to cool.

Roll out $\frac{1}{2}$ lb. almond paste thinly, cut out 5 heart shapes to fit top of cake and put in a warm place overnight to harden. Make up 1 lb. glacé icing, use half to coat the cake. Tint the rest pink, use most of it to coat the hearts separately. Reserve some in a closely covered container for the piped decorations. When icing is firm arrange the hearts on top of the cake, fixed with dabs of icing. Tint rest of icing darker pink, and pipe small stars round the outlines of the hearts and with the same tube pipe a line round the outer edge of each heart. Tie a bow of pink ribbon and fix to edge of cake with icing. Stand cake on a 12-inch silver board.

This type of raised decoration could be used for an unusual cake for a bridge party. The biscuits could be cut with fancy cutters in the shape of hearts, diamonds, spades and clubs, and applied to the top of the cake in the same way. Eight biscuits, two of each would be needed using the standard sized cutters.

**Above—Five Hearts Cake: the hearts are cut out of almond paste, and separately iced, then applied to the finished top of the cake and decorated with stars and line piping to cover up any uneven edges**

Brown & Polson

**Left—Valentine Heart Cake: to get a professional finish, trace off a heart shape smaller than that of the tins onto card, cut out and use as a template. Prick round it, taking care to position it evenly on the top of the cake and not to crack the glacé icing with the pin. Trim $\frac{1}{2}$-inch off the template all round and use as a guide again for inner circle of dots**

Cadbury Typhoo Food
Advisory Service

71

## THISTLE CAKE

*Make up Battenburg Cake Mixture in a 9 × 6-inch loaf tin (see p. 123).*

Coat with almond paste and place the cake join side down on a wire tray ready for icing. Put 10 oz. icing sugar in a saucepan, add a squeeze of lemon juice and enough warm water to make a coating consistency. Beat well, stir over a gentle heat for 1 minute. Coat the cake with the icing using a wet palette knife to smooth it. When set, decorate the cake with a thistle, using a large mauve pastille sweet for the body of the thistle and very thin strips of angelica for the top and sprays of leaves around. Finish the ends with trellis work, using a small writing tube, and tinting half the icing mauve and half green. Pipe alternate groups of verticals and horizontals in green and mauve, to simulate tartan.

**Top Left—Thistle Cake:** this attractive design makes it perfect for Burns Night, for St. Andrew's Day, even a Hogmanay celebration. Nicer still, make it as a treat for a Scottish friend's birthday

McDougalls Cookery Service

**Lower Left—Book Cake:** the decoration of "book" cakes can be much more elaborate if both time and skill permit. Try to copy a real book of your choice, possibly tracing off a scene from a greetings card to reproduce on the cover

Brown & Polson

72

## TRADITIONAL SIMNEL CAKE

*Make up Simnel Cake Mixture (see p. 119).*

Prepare and line an 8-inch cake tin. Put half the mixture into the tin and hollow out the centre slightly. Make up 1½ lb. almond paste, divide into 2 pieces, one a little larger than the other. Roll out the smaller one into a round the size of the cake tin and put it over the cake mixture, pressing down in the centre slightly. Add the rest of the cake mixture and smooth again, hollowing out centre about ½-inch. Bake for 2½ hours on middle shelf in a moderate oven for first hour, then reduce heat to slow for rest of cooking time.

When the cake is cold, divide the remaining almond paste into two. Roll out one piece into a round to fit the top of the cake. Brush the top of the cake with a little apricot jam and put on the round of almond paste. Roll remainder of paste into tiny balls, brush the edge of the almond paste with beaten egg and put all the paste balls round the edge close together, then brush with beaten egg. If liked, work a little paste into a thin rope and form a ring in the centre of the cake in the same way. Tie a piece of greaseproof paper round the cake, put it on a baking sheet and place in a moderate oven for 10-15 minutes to brown the top slightly.

Remove paper and when cold pour a little glacé icing into the centre and allow to set. Use Easter egg sweets and a fluffy chicken as decorations.

## BOOK CAKE

Make up the following cake mixture:— sift together 7½ oz. plain flour, 1 packet vanilla flavoured cornflour and 3 level teaspoonfuls baking powder. Beat 6 oz. butter and 5 oz. castor sugar together until soft and creamy, add the dry ingredients alternately with 3 well-beaten eggs. Add a little milk if necessary. Divide mixture between 2 6×9-inch greased tins, and bake for 20-25 minutes

McDougalls Cookery Service

**Simnel Cake: a real traditional recipe makes this the kind of rich fruit cake everyone enjoys at Easter, with a rich layer of almond paste baked inside it, a border of almond paste balls on top**

in a moderately hot oven. (Or use same tin twice.)

Make up 1 lb. almond paste, roll out thinly and use to cover the cake. Sandwich the two layers together with jam, brush over outside with warmed, sieved jam, and cover with the almond paste, leaving the front edge and two ends uncovered. Dent covered side with edge of ruler to resemble cover of book. Coat the top and back of the cake with royal icing and allow to set. Tint a little more icing pink and spread around the edges of the "book", roughing with a fork to form "leaves". Mount the cake on a suitable silver board, and decorate top and back of "book" with appropriate greeting and some small silver ornaments. (If liked a ribbon "marker" can be inserted near the back or spine of the book with diagonal cut end, or spray of flowers pinned to end.)

Party Engine Cake: you will be well rewarded for the time spent in making
this novelty by the realistic appearance and the pleasure it gives children

## PARTY ENGINE CAKE

*Required for the cakes: 6 oz. Table Margarine; 6 oz.
castor sugar; 3 eggs; 6 oz. s.r. flour; 2 heaped tablespoonfuls warm apricot jam.*
*Required for decorations: about 1½ lb. Satin Icing
(see p. 22), half only tinted red with food colouring;
1 large round chocolate biscuit; 1 large round cake
board; 4 oz. desiccated coconut; 2 thin pieces
angelica or 2 wooden cocktail sticks; ¼ lb. assorted
sweets; 8 small biscuits suitable for wheels; apricot
jam; small piece cotton wool.*

To make the cakes: brush the inside of a
12 × 8-inch swiss roll tin and a 6-inch square
cake tin with melted Table Margarine. Line
the swiss roll tin with a sheet of greaseproof
paper to cover above the sides of tin. Cream
the Table Margarine and sugar together in a
mixing bowl until light and fluffy. Beat in
the eggs, one at a time, adding a little of the
sieved flour with the second. Fold in the
remaining sieved flour. Place ⅔ of the mixture
in the swiss roll tin and the remaining ⅓ in

the square tin. Smooth over evenly. Bake in
a pre-heated fairly hot oven, the swiss roll on
second shelf from the top for 10-12 minutes,
and the square tin on the middle shelf for
15-20 minutes.

Turn out the swiss roll and fill with apricot
jam in the usual way. Turn out square cake
and cool, on a cake tray.

To make the truck: trim the outside edge
of the square cake with a sharp knife until
even. Cut in half; take one half, cut out the
centre and remove leaving a border ½-inch
wide of cake all round. Put the piece from
the centre to one side to be used later. Put the
half of cake, with hole in centre, on top of
the other half, and sandwich together with
apricot jam (see diagram 1).

To make the engine: Trim ends of swiss
roll until even. Cut out the cabin. Trim the
cut piece to go on top of the cabin "roof"
(see diagram 2). Make the cabin "step" and
the "funnels" from the cake cut away from

the truck (see diagram 3).

Roll out the red Satin Icing into an oblong, the same width as the swiss roll, and cut off the rough edges. Brush the roll with hot sieved apricot jam and cover with the prepared icing. Cover the "truck" in the same way. Cover the "funnels" with red and white Satin Icing (see photograph). Place the chocolate biscuit on the front of the "engine", securing with a little jam. Scatter desiccated coconut evenly over silver board. Place the "engine" and "truck" on top joining them together with 2 strips of angelica or 2 cocktail sticks.

Use small biscuits for the wheels, placing 2 on each side of the engine and 2 on each side of the truck. Press firmly against the Satin Icing so that they adhere to it. Gather

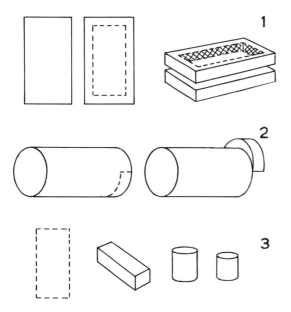

Modern Woman

## EASTER BUNNY CAKE

*Make up Sponge Mixture No. 1 (see p. 124) in an 8 × 12-inch swiss roll tin: quantities increased by ½.*

When cold cut carefully into shape shown in photograph. The base of the ears comes half-way down the cake, so trim round a plate of 7-inch diameter for the shape of the face up to the base of the ears on each side and mark central point between ears on same circle. Cut out deep inverted "v" from centre of top edge of cake down to point marked for base of ears and trim ears to points.

Make up 1 lb. stiff white glacé icing and use to cover the cake, reserving a few tablespoonfuls to be coloured pink for the insides of ears. Cover the cake with icing and dredge thickly with coarse-cut coconut. Cover over centres of ears with pink icing.

Arrange cake on a board. Outline eyes and mouth with narrow strips of licorice, tie wider licorice "bow" at base of neck, fill in eyes and nose with sweets, make whiskers of angelica.

together all the remaining red Satin Icing, roll out and cut 4 long strips about ½ an inch wide for the rails and a number of short strips for the sleepers. Arrange them on the desiccated coconut as shown in the photograph opposite to make a circular track round the cake board, hiding the joins under the engine and truck.

To make Marshmallow Snowmen: snip small piece off base of a pink marshmallow and press on to white marshmallow (damping if necessary) and secure with half wooden cocktail stick. Pink one is "head", white one is "body". Snip remaining white marshmallow into quarters and press tacky ends on to "body" for arms and legs. Press 3 cloves into body for buttons and 2 into face for eyes. Cut small triangles from glacé cherries and press into face for nose. Make dunce's caps from foil securing ends with Sellotape. Stand men round side of cake

## MARSHMALLOW SNOWMEN CAKE

*Make up Sponge Mixture No. 1 (see p. 124) in 2 7-inch sandwich tins, and sandwich together with strawberry jam.*

Make up a chocolate cream icing as follows:—Combine 2 oz. cocoa powder and 6 tablespoonfuls hot water, cook gently till the mixture thickens. Cream 4 oz. butter, and gradually blend in 10 oz. sieved icing sugar. Stir in cocoa mixture, beat well.

Swirl icing over top and sides of cake using knife blade to make decorative pattern.

Make up 8 marshmallow snowmen. You will need 3 marshmallows for each man (1 pink, 2 white), 5 cloves, tiny piece of glacé cherry and hat made from half-circle of coloured foil. (Pinch in half-circle at centre of straight side and bring straight sides one over the other to form a dunce's cap, then fasten with Sellotape.)

Mark off sides into 8 sections, and put one snowman against side of cake in each.

If you prefer, arrange the snowmen in a ring round the top edge of the cake, and if the cake is for a children's party, make sure there's a snowman available for each child.

Pascall Marshmallows

## SACK CAKE

*Make up Eggless Fruit Mixture (see p. 119) in a 5-inch round tin, lined high above edge with greaseproof paper. Bake in a slow oven on middle shelf for 1¼ hours.*

Make almond paste coating as follows:— sieve together 12 oz. ground almonds, 4 oz. castor sugar, 4 oz. icing sugar. Add 7 tablespoonfuls Nestlé's Condensed Milk, ¼ teaspoon vanilla essence, 3 drops almond essence, 1 teaspoonful lemon juice or 3 drops lemon essence. Mix thoroughly with a wooden spoon, press together with the hands into a ball and knead well. Roll out to a large circle, stand the cake on it and mould it up round the sides of the cake, making a nice roll at the top to resemble a sack opening. Coat with glacé icing. Tie a ribbon round the neck of the "sack". Fill centre with gold-wrapped chocolate money, mount cake on a 9-inch silver board and surround with birthday candles in holders fixed to board with icing. Be careful to space the candles out evenly before fixing them in place, and if liked heap some more chocolate money on the board as though it had spilled out of the sack.

## CANDLE CAKE

*Make up Swiss Roll Mixture (see p. 124).*

Make a filling by beating 2 level teaspoonfuls Nescafé, 2 oz. butter and 4 oz. sieved icing sugar, till mixture becomes light and creamy. Fill swiss roll and stand cake on end.

Roll out ½ lb. almond paste to cover the cooled swiss roll, having first brushed the surface with egg white. Allow to harden, coat with royal icing and smooth to candle shape with a wet palette knife. Run small amounts of icing down sides to represent melted candle wax. Colour small piece of almond paste with red colouring and shape into a flame for the top of the candle. Rough the surface round the bottom of the cake, and mount on a 6-inch board. If made for a birthday, ring the cake with the required number of candles and fresh flowers.

Nestlé's Cookery Service

Cadbury Typhoo Food Advisory Service

**Teddy Bears' Picnic Cake: little icing is needed on this cake, as cut-outs of marzipan teddy bears form a decoration**

## TEDDY BEARS' PICNIC CAKE

*Make up Fruit Cake Mixture No. 1 (see p. 120) in a deep 7-inch tin.*

Make up 1½ lb. almond paste, knead until smooth and pliable. Colour about 4 oz. paste yellow and remainder pale green. Roll out yellow paste to a thickness of ⅛-inch. From this cut out 20 teddy bear shapes with a fancy cutter. Put into a warm place to dry slightly. Spread a thin layer of sieved jam over top and around sides of cake, build up top edge of cake with pieces of green paste until level. Use rest to coat cake in usual way. Roll trimmings into a long strip ½-inch wide and place round base of cake. Decorate edge by fluting with fingers.

Arrange teddy bears, 5 evenly spaced on top and remainder round sides, and stick in place with glacé icing. With a No. 2 writing tube and chocolate glacé icing, pipe in buttons, eyes and mouths of bears and loop pattern round top edge, between bears, and round bottom edge of almond paste. Put a chocolate drop in centre of cake.

## CLOCK BIRTHDAY CAKE

*Make up Chocolate Sponge Mixture (see p. 126), dividing between a 6-inch sandwich tin and a 7-inch square tin.*

Mix 6 oz. sieved icing sugar with warm water to make a glacé icing and use to cover the round cake. Make up another 6 oz. sugar with a level teaspoonful instant coffee powder and water to a coffee glacé icing and use to cover the square cake, reserving a little for piping. Mix this with 1 level teaspoonful cocoa (and more sugar to stiffen if necessary)

Brown & Polson

**Clock Birthday Cake: pipe hands of clock pointing to show the child's age, and you need not put candles on this cake**

and using a No. 2 writing tube pipe in the numerals and hands of the clock. Mark off top into 4, and using these points as a guide, pipe in the numerals 12, 3, 6 and 9 first. Fill in the rest of the numerals, spacing them out evenly. The minute hand of the clock should point to 12, the hour hand should indicate the age of the child.

## CHOIR BOY CAKE

*Make up Eggless Fruit Cake Mixture, doubling the quantities (see p. 119) in a tall round food tin (body) and small basin (head).*

Make up 1½ lb. eggless almond paste (see p. 77). Stand tall cake on a board, cut away at top to form sloping shoulders. Coat with warm jam and cover with thin layer of almond paste, then with royal icing. Tint rest of paste flesh colour (with red and yellow food colouring). Trim small cake round, cover with pink almond paste. Trim small paper bun case to form collar, place on top of tall cake and with a little icing fix "head" in centre of bun case. Make "face" with 2 blobs of icing centred with currants for "eyes", ring of glacé cherry for "mouth" and 2 tiny spots of cherry for "nose". Cover top of head with very stiff royal icing. When it sets, with a sharp knife cut zig-zag fringe round forehead. With trimmings of pink almond paste form 2 hands, stick to centre of body with icing, surrounding with "frill" of icing. Mount on a 6-inch silver board, pipe shell border round base with No. 12 ribbon tube. Decorate with various coloured mimosa balls. Fix candle holders to edge of board with icing. Fix narrow red or purple ribbon round neck to fall down either side of hands to base.

Stork Cookery Service

## ROCKET CAKE

*Make up Swiss Roll Mixture (see p. 124). Finish by filling with raspberry jam.*

To make a glacé fudge icing, melt 2 oz. Table Margarine and 3 dessertspoonfuls orange juice in a saucepan. Remove from heat, add 8 oz. sieved icing sugar, and beat well until cool. Stand the swiss roll on one end. Cover with fudge icing and mark in grooves with a fork. Position on a 9-inch silver board with a little white glacé icing, take out to cover board to edge and before icing is dry, sprinkle with coconut tinted green. Make face and ears with almond paste tinted red, and small sweets. Cut 3 "fins" and a circle 6 inches in diameter from coloured paper. Fix "fins" round sides, cut

Nestlé's Cookery Service

circle through to centre and fold cut edges one over the other and fix with Sellotape to make a hat. Surround base of cake on board with small fireworks.

## VALENTINE COFFEE CAKE

*Make up Coffee Sponge Mixture (see p. 124) in an 8-inch heart-shaped tin.*

Make up a coffee butter cream by beating 5 oz. butter until smooth and soft, then stir in 8 oz. icing sugar and 3 tablespoonfuls strong black coffee. Cut the cake in half and sandwich with butter cream. Spread some over the top and sides to cover, and colour the rest darker with a little more coffee. With a No. 8 star tube pipe small stars round top edge, down point of heart, and round bottom edge of cake. Pipe another heart outline in stars leaving an inch-wide border inside the edge. Fill this with cracked caramel.

To make the caramel, dissolve 4 oz. loaf sugar in 1 gill water, then boil rapidly until dark golden brown. Pour out of saucepan immediately onto a sheet of greaseproof paper and leave to cool and harden. Crack with a rolling-pin and use to decorate the top of the cake.

## MOTHER'S DAY CAKE

(Colour Plate No. 15)

*Make up Fruit Cake Mixture No. 1 (see p. 120) and bake in an 8-inch round tin.*

Cover the cake with 1½ lb. almond paste. Make up 1½ lb. Fondant Icing (see p. 22). Colour pale yellow. Brush the almond paste covering the cake with a little egg white. Roll out the fondant icing on a board sprinkled with cornflour to approximately 12 inches in diameter. Place over the top of the cake with fingers dipped in cornflour. Trim the icing at the base. Place on a silver board covered with a gold doily. Using a No. 2 writing tube, pipe "Mother" in yellow glacé icing. Tie a narrow ribbon around the base and if liked arrange two yellow roses on top of the cake.

As an alternative design for a Mother's Day Cake, make up some extra fondant icing and work in yellow food colouring to make the fondant a deeper yellow than that used to cover the cake. Following the instructions on pages 30-1, make some moulded roses. When dry, group the roses on the surface of the cake. Add a few sprigs of fern to complete the decoration.

## BUNNY RING CAKE

(Colour Plate No. 16)

*Make up Sponge Mixture No. 2 (see p. 124) in a 9-inch sandwich tin.*

Cream together 8 oz. well-sieved icing sugar, and 4 oz. superfine margarine, till light and fluffy. Add a few drops vanilla essence and mix in well. Spread top and sides of cake with icing and smooth with a wet palette knife. Reserve a little for the "tails" of the bunnies.

Add sap green colouring to 8 oz. coarse-cut coconut and work it in with the finger tips until uniformly coloured. Using a knife, work tinted coconut up and round sides of cake. Sprinkle coconut evenly on top and press lightly with the blade of a knife. Drain syrup from a large tin of Bartlett pears, decorate them with cloves for the eyes and toasted halved almonds for ears. Arrange pears on top of cake (fitting in close together with stalk ends inwards, either 7 or 8 according to size of pears). Trim them slightly if necessary.

Position small pieces of glacé cherry to represent tongues and lastly pipe rosettes of icing to represent tails.

**Mother's Day Cake: a rich fruit cake covered with pale yellow fondant icing and decorated with delicate matching roses and ribbon**

Plate 15

Simnel Wreath Cake: thin ropes of almond paste are coiled together to make an effective edge to the cake and, in a much smaller version, a "nest" for the centre of the cake where a fluffy chick can perch on a nest of "eggs"

Brown & Polson

Bunny Ring Cake: well-drained tinned pears can easily be made to look like bunnies when arranged on coconut tinted green, as if they were nibbling away on a grassy lawn together . . . ears are made of toasted almonds and the fluffy tails piped on with cream in stars

Kraft Foods

Plate 16

**Right**—Broken Egg Chick Cake: an Easter novelty with a simple decoration using a small chocolate egg and a few chocolate drops. Mark the exact shape you want with a pointed knife first so that the egg breaks apart leaving one-third in a neat shape to lay on top of the icing as a nest

Cadbury Typhoo Food Advisory Service

**Below**—Coffee Easter Gâteau: a delicate sponge filled and topped with coffee-flavoured butter cream and icing has a delicious coating of toasted coconut and a ring of chicks ready to peck at the centre circle of coconut, all outlined with rings of stars

Coffee Information Bureau

Plate 17

**Cranberry Cut-out Cake:**
A group of jolly little bears
cut out of cranberry jelly
slices hold the strings of
gay balloons (moulded from
coloured almond paste)

Cranberry Kitchen

**Square Rabbit Cake:** A
frieze of marzipan rabbits is
used to decorate this cake
with a piped border of
"grass" and flower heads at
the corners made of crystallised violets

Plate 18

# CRANBERRY CUT-OUT CAKE

(Colour Plate No. 18)

*Make up Whisked Sponge Mixture No. 1 (see p. 124) in 2 7-inch sandwich tins.*

Make up ¾ lb. butter cream, flavoured with a few drops of vanilla essence. Chill a 7 oz. tin jellied cranberry sauce, and turn out carefully. Cut three ¼-inch thick slices; then, with a standard teddy-bear cutter, cut out three teddy bears. Lay on soft kitchen paper to dry out, and store in the refrigerator.

Beat the remainder of the jelly into about ⅓ of the butter cream and use the cranberry flavoured cream to sandwich the 2 cakes together. Smooth the rest of the butter cream on top and round the sides of the cake, marking the sides with a fork. Let icing harden for an hour or so. Position cake on a 9-inch cake board with icing.

Make faces for the bears with silver balls and lay the teddy bears in position across centre of cake. Place 3 flattened circles of coloured marzipan or large flat sweets in place to represent balloons. With a little chocolate glacé icing and a No. 1 writing tube, pipe in strings for the balloons and an edging round the base of the cake. (With the aid of different shaped cutters or designs of your own, different cut-outs can be made from the jelly for quick and easy cake decoration.)

# SQUARE RABBIT CAKE

(Colour Plate No. 18)

*Make up Rich Chocolate Cake Mixture (see p. 126) in a square 7-inch tin.*

Make up ¾ lb. glacé icing tinted pale pink with cochineal, reserving a little to tint green for piping. Coat the cake with the rest of the icing and allow to set firmly. Mount on a 9-inch board with a dab of icing. Make up about ½ lb. almond paste and tint brown with food colouring, working it in evenly. Roll out on a sugared board and cut out 10 small rabbit shapes. Press two of these against each side of the cake, and two on top

in a diagonal line from corner to corner.

Using the remaining icing stiffened with a little more icing sugar and tinted green with food colouring, and a No. 2 writing tube, pipe a border of "grass" round the top and bottom edges of the cake and pipe round top edge again in a looped border to make a neat finish. Pipe "grass" on either side of the 2 rabbits on top, and fix tiny flower-heads made of crystallised violets to the corners and corner sides of cake.

# SIMNEL WREATH CAKE

(Colour Plate No. 16)

*Make up Simnel Wreath Cake Mixture (see p. 119). Prepare an 8-inch round cake tin.*

Make up 1-1½ lb. almond paste, roll about half of it into a circle to fit the tin. Put half the cake mixture in the tin, cover with the round of almond paste, then with the remainder of the cake mixture. Bake 2½-3 hours in a moderate oven. When cool, roll ⅔ of the rest of the paste into a round to fit the top of the cake. Fit this into place, smoothing down over the edge to make a wide border about an inch deep down the sides of the cake.

Make 2 coils with the remaining paste, 1 large one to fit round edge, and a smaller one for the centre. Press in place, brush with egg white and brown under the grill. When cold fill the centre with Easter egg sweets, and add 2 fluffy chicks to decorate.

# BROKEN EGG CHICK CAKE

(Colour Plate No. 17)

*Make up Chocolate Sponge Mixture (see p. 126) in 2 7-inch sandwich tins.*

Make up sufficient butter cream to fill and coat the cake generously. Add almond flavouring to taste, and tint ⅓ pale green for top of cake. Use remainder to sandwich the two cakes together and to coat the sides smoothly. Roll the cake in flaked almonds to coat the sides evenly.

Decorate the top with the remaining butter cream, swirling with a knife blade. Break a small chocolate Easter egg in two, using the smaller half as a "nest" for one or two fluffy chicks and finish with about 20 chocolate buttons pressed into the icing, leading down from either side of the egg to the edge of the cake and all round the top edge to meet at the back.

## COFFEE EASTER GÂTEAU
(Colour Plate No. 17)

*Make up Coffee Sponge Mixture (see p. 124) in 2 7-inch sandwich tins.*

Make up a coffee butter cream by beating 5 oz. butter until smooth and soft, then stir in 8 oz. icing sugar and 3 tablespoonfuls strong black coffee. Use to sandwich the 2 cakes together and to cover the sides, reserving a little for piping. Roll sides in desiccated coconut, toasted pale brown in the oven.

Cover the top of the cake with coffee glacé icing and leave to set. With a No. 8 star tube pipe a border of rosettes round the top edge of the cake and a small circle of 1½-inch diameter in the centre. Fill this with more toasted coconut. Arrange four fluffy chicks round this circle. Or decorate the cake by putting a mound of Easter Egg sweets inside the circle of rosettes instead.

## S.S. BOYTOWN CAKE

*Make up Simnel Wreath Cake Mixture (see p. 119) in a 7-inch round tin.*

Make up 1 lb. almond paste and coat the cake in the usual way. Make up 1½ lb. royal icing and use to coat the cake, reserving a little to tint pale blue with food colouring for base of cake. Coat sides and an inch-wide

**Right—S.S. Boytown Cake: iced biscuits make the lifebelts round the sides of the cake, chocolate boats float on top**

border on top of a 9-inch cake board with blue icing, place round cake in position on this, fork up blue icing still showing on top of board to represent "sea".

Make 8 round biscuits with centres cut out with smaller cutter from 4 o'clock Biscuit Dough (see p. 98). Coat one side with blue glacé icing. Fill 5 greased boat-shaped tins with chocolate melted in a double boiler or basin over hot water and turn out when set. With chocolate glacé icing and No. 1 writing tube, pipe "S.S. BOYTOWN" round the iced biscuits, and names on triangular paper sails for the boats. Fix sails in position with wooden cocktail sticks and arrange biscuits round sides of cake with dabs of icing and boats on top of cake.

## MAYPOLE BIRTHDAY CAKE

*Make up Chocolate Cake Mixture (see p. 126) in a 7-inch round tin.*

Stand the cake on a 9-inch board. Make up about 1¼ lb. icing sugar with 2 egg whites to a stiff paste, and knead in sufficient cochineal to give a pale pink colour. Spread a thin layer of sieved jam over the top and round the sides of the cake. Use half the flat icing, knead into a smooth ball and roll into a circle to fit the top of the cake. Roll into

Brown & Polson

position. Divide the remainder into two strips each to fit half-way round the sides of the cake. Seal well. Make up ½ lb. royal icing of piping consistency.

Divide top of cake into as many sections as candles are required. Space out candles evenly in holders round top of cake, and make hole in centre with skewer to take a coloured straw for "maypole". With No. 21 star tube pipe rosettes round top edge and

Stork Cookery Service

**Above—Easter Bonnet Cake: frilled brim is made by pleating a strip of Satin Icing to fit round the edge of the cake plate**

**Left—Maypole Birthday Cake: favourite cut-outs from a book mounted on thin card are used to fasten ribbons to the sides**

Cadbury Typhoo Food Advisory Service

base of cake and shells round edge of board. Make as many 1½-inch square cut-outs of coloured pictures glued to thin board as there are candles, and fix with icing to sides of cake between candles. Fix ribbons of various colours from top of "maypole" to back of each cut-out, fixing with dabs of icing. Pipe a border of small rosettes with No. 6 star tube round each cut-out. Top "maypole" with a chocolate button held in place with a dab of icing and a pin.

## EASTER BONNET

*Make up Swiss Roll Mixture (see p. 124) in an 8-inch sandwich tin.*

Make up 1½ lb. icing sugar into Stork Satin Icing (see recipe and method on p. 22). Brush the top and sides of the cake with hot sieved apricot jam. Roll out ⅓ of the Satin Icing into a round large enough to cover the cake top. Trim off any surplus icing. Roll out a long strip deep enough to cover sides of cake, trim to fit. Roll up like a bandage, then use to cover sides of cake. Roll out the remaining Satin Icing into a long strip rather more thinly, about 1½ times circumference of cake, and 1 inch wide. Trim with a pastry wheel or knife to give pinked edge along one side for hat "frill".

Pleat it or fold it round the outside edge of a 9-inch cake board and place the cake in the centre. Tie a narrow ribbon round the cake in a bow and decorate the top with sprigs of artificial flowers and any other small decorations preferred. Take care to serve a portion of the marzipan "frill" with each slice of cake so that it is not wasted.

## HONEYBREAD HOUSE CAKE

Make up Honeybread Mixture as follows:
—cream ½ lb. butter with ½ lb. moist brown sugar until light and fluffy. Add ½ pint warmed milk, 4 level tablespoonfuls Gale's clear honey and ¼ lb. black treacle. Beat up 2 eggs and add to mixture. Sieve together 1 lb. plain flour, 1 teaspoonful each ground ginger, mixed spice and bicarbonate of soda, and beat well into mixture until smooth. Stir in ½ lb. California seedless raisins. Pour into a greased and bottom-lined cake tin 8½ × 6½ × 2½ inches, bake in cool oven for 2¼ hours or until firm to touch. Cool on wire tray.

Make up about 1 lb. royal icing. To make the house, cut cake in half, sandwich pieces

The Honey Bureau

together with royal icing and stand on edge. Shape roof by cutting off triangular wedges. Add extra height to roof by placing wedges together on top. Spread the sides of cake with royal icing. Roll out 1 lb. almond paste thinly into a rectangle, trim edges and place on cake to form roof. Shape remaining almond paste into small rectangles for windows and door. Press against sides of cake. Form timbers, shutters and door knocker with strips of angelica and paint "panes" in windows with brown food colouring. Mark "thatching" on roof with back of knifeblade.

## GYPSY CARAVAN CAKE

*Make up Honeybread Mixture as for Honeybread House Cake in a 2 lb. loaf tin.*

Make up about 1 lb. almond paste. Brush the cake with warm apricot jam. Roll out almond paste and shape one piece to fit top of cake, press on firmly. Roll out rest of paste into a strip to go round sides of cake and press into place. Leave to dry out overnight. Cut thin board exactly to fit base, mount cake on this. Make up 1½ lb. royal icing. Coat four large round biscuits with some of this, and the cake. Stand cake on 2 small upturned jars. Press small candle into "roof" to form chimney. Tint rest of icing any pastel shade desired, and using No. 3 writing tube pipe in rim and spokes of wheels and panelling on body of caravan. With star tube No. 6 pipe rosettes round edge of roof, base of cake, wheel hubs, sides of windows and scrolls at each corner of roof. Press wheels against sides of cake to fix in position, and make "shafts" of angelica. (If no toy horse is available, stand the caravan on a cake board covered with desiccated coconut tinted green.)

California Raisin Bureau

84

# Other Cakes

# and Gâteaux

## BUTTERFLY WINGS CAKE

*Make up Sponge Mixture No. 2 (see p. 124) in 2 7-inch sandwich tins.*

Put 2 packets of Kraft Philadelphia Cream Cheese Spread into a basin with 20 oz. icing sugar and 4 dessertspoonfuls lemon juice. Beat together until smooth and just able to pour. Use about ⅔ of this to sandwich the two cakes together, and to cover. Place cake on a wire tray over a plate and pour over the icing, spreading with a palette knife. Add a little more icing sugar to remainder to ensure firm piping consistency, and reserve for decorating. Allow cake to harden, keeping rest of icing covered with a damp cloth. Mark off top of cake into 12 sections.

Using a No. 8 star tube pipe straight lines dividing the sections, and another line all round the edge of the cake. Fill each alternate section with Black Raspberry and Pineapple Preserves. Overpipe the lines with the same

tube and fill centre with a large rosette.

Transfer cake to serving plate and with same tube pipe a line round the base, doubling with the tube every inch. Have ready 6 ice-cream wafers cut diagonally from corner to corner. Insert half a wafer at an angle between each line of piping and the Preserves next to it, to give the effect of butterfly wings.

**Butterfly Wings Cake: taken step by step, the decoration is really very simple to do**

**Pineapple Party Gâteau: flavoured corn-flour gives delicate texture and taste to this luscious-looking and creamy Gâteau**

## PINEAPPLE PARTY GÂTEAU

Make up the following Pineapple Sponge:—separate 3 eggs and beat the whites stiffly with a pinch of salt. Add the yolks and continue beating until the mixture is thick and creamy. Add 4 oz. castor sugar gradually, beating all the time, until the mixture is thick enough to leave a trail. Carefully fold in 1 oz. Patent Cornflour and 1 pkt. Pineapple Flavoured Cornflour sifted together, and turn into 2 8-inch greased sandwich tins. Bake about 20 minutes in a moderately hot oven.

Sandwich the sponge cakes together with Pineapple Preserves. Open and drain a small tin of pineapple rings. Mix a little syrup from tin with more warmed jam and brush round sides of cake. Trim boudoir biscuits to come with rounded ends $\frac{1}{2}$-inch above edge of cake and stick in place closely side by side. Secure by tying narrow ribbon round cake in a bow. Halve 4 pineapple slices and arrange radiating out from centre of cake. Whip $\frac{1}{4}$ pt. double cream, and with No. 8 star tube, pipe stars all over top of cake, and a large rosette in the centre.

Place one glacé cherry in centre, and one in each section near edge, flanked by diamond-shaped wings of angelica. Serve on a border of leaves, with a "bunch" of glacé cherries at one side.

## ONE-STAGE FRUIT GÂTEAU

Make up one-stage cake as follows:—put all together in a mixing bowl the following ingredients—1 $\frac{1}{4}$ lb. packet Luxury Margarine; 4 oz. castor sugar; 2 eggs; 4 oz. s.r. flour and 1 level teaspoonful baking powder sieved together. Beat well for one minute with a wooden spoon. Divide between 2 7-inch sandwich tins, previously brushed with melted Luxury Margarine and bottom-lined

with greaseproof paper. Bake on middle shelf of a very moderate oven for 25-35 minutes. Cool on wire rack.

Drain the juice from a medium tin of peach slices. Whisk up $\frac{1}{4}$ pt. of double cream until stiff. Spread $\frac{3}{4}$ of the cream on one sandwich cake, and place a layer of fruit on top, keeping back a few slices for decoration. Place the other cake on this and sprinkle with icing sugar. Spoon the remaining cream into a heap in the centre. Decorate with halved peach slices, and one glacé cherry surrounded by leaves of angelica in the centre.

NOTE: Quite elaborate looking gâteaux can be built up on the basis of a simple cake by filling and decorating with whipped cream and well-drained tinned fruit. Unless the cake is to be served at once, it is advisable to glaze the fruit with a sugar syrup thickened as desired with arrowroot.

Blue Band Bureau

Right—Raspberry Butterfly Cake: sponge sandwich with top layer split and reset as wings

Opposite—One-Stage Fruit Gâteau: the basic sponge filled and topped with fruit and cream

Below—Oranges and Lemons Cake: crystallised slices decorate a glacé-iced chocolate cake

## RASPBERRY BUTTERFLY CAKE

Make up same basic cake as for One-Stage Fruit Gâteau in a deeper 8-inch tin, baking for 35-45 minutes as deeper cake takes longer to cook.

Whisk up $\frac{1}{4}$ pt. of double cream until stiff and prepare $\frac{1}{2}$ lb. fresh raspberries or loganberries. Cut the cooled cake through the centre. Spread or pipe half the cream on the bottom half, place the fruit on top building up on opposite sides away from centre of cake, reserving 3 berries for top. Cut the top half of the cake in two and place on top of fruit to form "wings". Sprinkle with icing sugar. Pipe rosettes of cream down the centre to mask join and decorate with fruit.

## ORANGES AND LEMONS CAKE
(Colour Plate No. 13)

*Make up Chocolate Sponge Mixture (see p. 126) in 2 7-inch sandwich tins.*

Cream together 2 oz. butter and 4 oz. icing sugar until well blended. Squeeze the juice from a large orange and reserve for the glacé icing. Remove flesh from the skin and beat into the butter cream. Use to sandwich the two sponge layers together. Sieve 6 oz. icing sugar and mix to a stiff consistency with the orange juice and a little warm water if necessary. Spread evenly over top of cake.

Allow the icing almost to set then decorate with crystallised orange and lemon slices, trimming them if necessary to exactly even sizes. You will need about 30 altogether. Place the slices with points inwards as close together as possible round top edge of cake, and with points downwards against sides of cake, making sure they adhere to the filling.

Cadbury Typhoo Food Advisory Service

## ICED BUTTERFLY CAKE

(Colour Plate No. 3)

*Make up Rich Chocolate Cake (see p. 126) in an 8-inch square tin.*

Place the cake on a board, and using a sharp knife cut it diagonally in half to form the 2 wings of a butterfly. Cut off 2 triangles from the opposite corners. Turn the triangles and place the 2 latter cut edges together. Cut out 2 more triangles from the diagonal edges directly opposite each other equal in size (about 2 inches).

Place the 2 wings on a wire tray and brush away any surplus crumbs. Make up a glacé icing, using 1½ lb. icing sugar and sufficient warm water to form a thick coating consistency. From this take about 2 tablespoonfuls of the mixture and place in a small basin. Blend 3 teaspoonfuls drinking chocolate with sufficient boiling water to dissolve it. Add to the small quantity of glacé icing to form a chocolate icing. Put into a piping bag made of greaseproof paper, but do not cut off end at this stage.

Ice each wing separately because it is important to carry through the following stages quickly before icing hardens. Pour half the white icing over one wing and spread evenly round sides. Quickly nip off end of piping bag and pipe lines parallel to long edge. Using a skewer immediately draw lines across the chocolate piping from a central point radiating out to the longer edge.

Repeat this process on the other wing. Allow to set before assembling. Arrange both wings on a square cake board. Mould 1 oz. marzipan into the shape of the body. Coat with seedless jam and dip in chocolate vermicelli. Place into position. Press 2 cloves into a sugared sweet for eyes and skewer into position with two pieces of bent wire for feelers. The wire used by florists is ideal for this purpose. Make ½ lb. royal icing and with a small star tube pipe shells round base of butterfly to neaten edge.

Cadbury Typhoo Food Advisory Service

## FLOWER BASKET CAKE

*Make up Fruit Cake Mixture No. 1 (see p. 120) in an 8-inch round tin.*

Make up 1½ lb. almond paste and use to coat the cake in the usual way, reserving 2 oz. for the marzipan flowers. Make up 1 lb. flat icing as follows:—mix 2 tablespoonfuls Bournville cocoa to a smooth paste with a little boiling water and allow to cool. Put 2 egg whites into a bowl and add sufficient icing sugar to form a stiff icing. Beat well. Add sufficient blended cocoa to obtain a pale chocolate colour. Take out about 2 tablespoonfuls of the mixture and add more blended cocoa to make a dark chocolate icing. Add a little more icing sugar if necessary to stiffen.

Put the darker icing into an icing bag or syringe with a No. 3 writing tube, and the paler icing into one with a No. 9 fancy band tube. First ice the sides of the cake. Work from left to right, alternately using the plain and then the fancy band tube. Pipe a line of dark icing straight down side of cake. Pipe inch-wide strips of basket work across this with the paler icing, leaving space exactly same width as each strip between the strips. Pipe another straight line of dark icing down the side of these strips, ½-inch away from and parallel to the first line. Fill in the alternate spaces with more inch-wide strips of basket work and repeat.

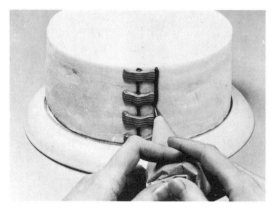

Cut a piece of cardboard exactly half the size of the cake top. Ice one half of the top in a similar way, but working from a central point so that strips of basket-work get wider towards outer edge. Pipe the same design onto the semi-circular piece of card. Finish off basket edges and allow to dry. Work pink food colouring into reserved almond paste and make about a dozen roses of various sizes and a few buds (see p. 30). Cut rose leaves from sheet angelica. Arrange roses and leaves on uncovered half of cake, prop cardboard "lid" up to give a basket effect.

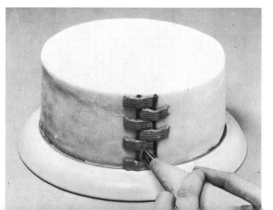

Cadbury Typhoo Food Advisory Service

Left—Tyrolean Ginger Cake: a very rich sweet ginger cake piped and filled with fresh cream makes a welcome change

Opposite—Flaming Cake: apricots make the cups holding sugar cubes soaked in lemon essence or brandy and set alight

Below—Iced Angel Cake: a delicate finish of pink and blue sugar flowers contrasts well with the white cake and icing

Brown & Polson

## TYROLEAN GINGER CAKE

Prepare a $7\frac{3}{4} \times 4\frac{3}{4} \times 3\frac{3}{4}$ inch cake tin by lining the bottom with paper and grease well all over. Sift together 9 oz. plain flour, $\frac{1}{2}$ level teaspoon salt, 2 level teaspoonfuls baking powder, 3 level teaspoonfuls ground ginger and $7\frac{1}{2}$ oz. soft brown sugar in a bowl. Mix together yolks of 3 eggs, $\frac{1}{4}$ pt. corn oil and $\frac{1}{4}$ pt. milk, and add to the dry ingredients. Beat the egg whites stiffly and fold in. Turn the mixture into the prepared tin and bake about 1 hour 40 minutes in a moderate oven. Turn out and leave to cool, then return to tin. Pierce all over with a skewer and pour on ginger syrup. Leave to soak overnight, then slice in half lengthways.

To make ginger syrup, boil 6 oz. castor sugar and $\frac{1}{2}$ pt. water together briskly for 5 minutes, remove from heat and stir in 4 table-spoonfuls syrup from a jar of preserved ginger.

Chop 4 oz. preserved ginger finely. Whip $\frac{1}{4}$ to $\frac{1}{2}$ pt. cream until stiff, use half of this mixed with the chopped ginger to fill the cake. Using a No. 14 star tube, pipe parallel

McDougalls Cookery Service

lines close together from left to right up end of cake, over top and down other end. Finish with rosettes across each end and two "fans" of preserved ginger.

## ICED ANGEL CAKE

Sieve together 2 oz. Super-Sifted s.r. flour and 4 oz. castor sugar twice. Whisk 4 egg whites with scant $\frac{1}{2}$ teaspoon cream of tartar until stiff. Using a metal spoon fold in care-

90

fully the sugar, flour and 1 coffeespoonful vanilla essence. Pour into an ungreased 7-inch tube tin and bake for 40 minutes in a cool oven, covering with greaseproof paper when sufficiently brown. Leave in tin until cold before removing.

Make up some Marshmallow Frosting (see p. 92). Place cake on wire rack over a plate and pour over the icing, smoothing with a knife. Allow several hours to set.

Make up a little stiff royal icing. Tint half of it pink and the other half pale blue with food colouring. Using the pink icing and No. 36 small rose tube, pipe out 5 roses on greaseproof paper. Using the blue icing and No. 42 small petal tube, pipe out 15 forget-me-nots on greaseproof paper. Put a tiny dot of white icing in the centre of each forget-me-not (see p. 30 for instructions for making sugar flowers).

Arrange the flowers in 5 groups of 1 rose and 3 forget-me-nots each, flanked by 2 diamond-shaped leaves of angelica.

## FLAMING CAKE

Prepare a 7-inch tube tin by greasing lightly. Sift together 6 oz. plain flour, 2 level teaspoonfuls baking powder, $\frac{1}{2}$ level teaspoon salt and 5 oz. castor sugar into a mixing bowl and add the grated rind of an orange. Mix together 2 egg yolks, $3\frac{1}{2}$ fl. oz. corn oil and the juice of the orange made up to $3\frac{1}{2}$ fl. oz. with water. Add to the dry ingredients. Beat well to form a smooth, slack mixture. Beat egg whites stiffly and fold in lightly. Turn mixture into the prepared tin and bake for about 50 minutes in a moderate oven.

When cold cover with Marshmallow Frosting (see next page). With knife blade swirl round top and up and down sides. Make tiny bows of orange and green narrow ribbon and press against sides of cake before icing is quite dry. Place drained tinned apricot halves round the top of the cake.

Put a small cube of sugar in each, add a few drops of lemon essence and set alight.

Brown & Polson

## GUIDE TO QUANTITIES OF GLACÉ ICING REQUIRED FOR DIFFERENT SIZED CAKES

| | |
|---|---|
| 6-in. diameter Top only | 5 oz. icing sugar, etc. |
| 6-in. diameter Top and sides | 10 oz. icing sugar, etc. |
| 7-in. diameter Top only | 6 oz. icing sugar, etc. |
| 7-in. diameter Top and sides | 12 oz. icing sugar, etc. |
| 8-in. diameter Top only | 8 oz. icing sugar, etc. |
| 8-in. diameter Top and sides | 16 oz. icing sugar, etc. |
| 9-in. diameter Top only | 8 oz. icing sugar, etc. |
| 9-in. diameter Top and sides | $1\frac{1}{4}$ lb. icing sugar, etc. |

**CUP CAKES**

| | |
|---|---|
| 12 tops only | 6 oz. icing sugar, etc. |

## MARSHMALLOW GARLAND CAKE

*Make up Whisked Sponge Mixture No. 1 (see p. 124) in 2 7-inch sandwich tins.*

Sandwich cakes together with strawberry jam. Make Marshmallow Frosting as follows:—melt 4 oz. (25) marshmallows slowly in 2 tablespoonfuls milk, then leave to cool, stirring occasionally. Beat 2 egg whites and 1 oz. castor sugar until stiff and peaky, fold into the marshmallow mixture. Leave to set a little before using.

Swirl the Marshmallow Frosting over the top and sides of the cake. When set place a garland of glazed nuts round the edge.

To glaze the nuts, make a sugar glaze as follows:—put 4 oz. sugar and 2 tablespoonfuls water into a pan, bring to boil stirring gently to dissolve sugar, then boil steadily without stirring over a medium heat until a small quantity of mixture forms a soft ball when dropped into cold water (if using a sugar thermometer, when it registers 240° F.). Dip about 20 assorted nuts into glaze and leave to set on greased greaseproof paper.

NOTE: It is much easier to make larger quantities of glaze, doubling or trebling the recipe, and it is very suitable for covering petits fours, such as marzipan stuffed dates, walnuts sandwiched together with marzipan, and black or white grapes. Small quantities of sugar glaze tend to turn easily.

**Marshmallow Frosting is soft and satiny, easily spread and covers well**

Pascall Marshmallows

92

Brown & Polson

Jamaica Ring: a delicate chocolate angel cake, filled and coated with a rich icing which incorporates butter and rum, is piped with whipped cream

## JAMAICA RING

Make up Chocolate Angel Cake as follows:—mix together 2 fl. oz. corn oil, 4 fl. oz. water and the yolks of 2 eggs. Add 5 oz. plain flour, 1 oz. cocoa, $5\frac{1}{2}$ oz. castor sugar and 2 level teaspoonfuls baking powder sifted together. Beat to form a smooth, slack batter. Beat up the egg white, a pinch of salt and $\frac{1}{4}$ level teaspoon cream of tartar very stiffly and fold into the batter lightly. Turn into an ungreased 8-inch savarin mould and bake about $1\frac{1}{4}$ hours in a slow oven.

Leave to cool in the tin for $\frac{1}{2}$ hour then turn out. When completely cool, split in half cross-wise. Sprinkle the cut surface of the lower half liberally with rum.

Make a chocolate filling and coating as follows:—mix 1 oz. cornflour, 8 oz. sugar and 2 egg yolks smoothly with a little taken from $\frac{1}{2}$ pt. cold water. Put the rest of the water on to heat with 4 oz. plain chocolate.

When the chocolate is completely melted, add the mixed cornflour and cook gently for 3 minutes, stirring constantly. Remove from the heat and stir in 1 oz. butter and 1 teaspoonful rum. Allow to cool thoroughly before using.

Sandwich the cake together with a layer of the chocolate mixture, and a layer of whipped cream. Spread the whole of the outside of the cake with the remainder of the chocolate mixture, smoothing with a knife blade. Allow to set. Put the rest of the whipped cream into a forcing bag or syringe with a No. 14 star tube and pipe a zig-zag pattern round the inner top edge of the ring. Place on a serving plate and pipe a similar zig-zag pattern round the base. Fill in the space under the inverted "v" patterns with rosettes, using same tube. Decorate the top of the cake with mimosa balls and long, narrow spikes of angelica, just before it sets.

93

Kraft Foods

**Gâteau aux Pêches: rosettes of cream are
used to outline glazed tinned peach halves**

## GÂTEAU AUX PÊCHES
(Colour Plate No. 20)

*Make up Sponge Mixture No. 2 (see p. 124) in 2
7-inch sandwich tins.*

Sandwich the cakes together with about
6 oz. Pure Peach Preserves. Beat up a $\frac{1}{4}$ pt.
carton of double cream until stiff enough for
piping. Cut 13 sponge fingers in half. Smear
the flat sides with cream, and arrange round
the outside of the cake. Open a $15\frac{1}{2}$ oz. tin of
half cling peaches.

Blend 1 teaspoonful arrowroot with a little
of the peach juice, and bring remainder to
the boil in a saucepan. Add to the arrowroot,
stir and return to the heat until it boils and
becomes clear, stirring continuously. Allow
to cool.

Place cake on serving plate. Well drain
the peach halves, and arrange six on top of
the cake, in a ring of 5 with 1 peach half in
the centre, cut sides down. Spoon the glaze
over them, taking care to coat completely.
When set, use a No. 14 star tube to pipe
rosettes of cream in groups of 3, separating
the peaches in the circle and filling in space
between them and the sponge biscuits. Finish
with rosettes between the bases of the biscuits
and tie a narrow ribbon round cake.

## MILLE FEUILLES GÂTEAU
(Colour Plate No. 20)

Make up 8 oz. puff pastry, and roll out
very thin, about the thickness of a penny.
Cut into 4 equal-sized rounds (using bottom
of 8-inch cake tin as guide). Put carefully on
to ungreased baking trays and bake for 10
minutes in a very hot oven, or until well risen.
If pastry seems underdone, turn off heat and
leave a few minutes more in oven. When
cold, sandwich layers with raspberry jam and
confectioner's custard, as follows.

**Mille Feuilles Gâteau: means literally
"A thousand leaves cake", is light as air**

Blend 2 level tablespoonfuls vanilla flavour
custard powder with $\frac{1}{2}$ pt. milk, put in a
saucepan and bring to boil gradually, with 1
tablespoonful castor sugar and 1 teaspoonful
vanilla essence, stirring all the time. Cook
until very thick, take off heat and cool for one
minute. Add 2 eggs, well beaten together, and
return to heat, stirring gently, for a few
minutes. Do not boil or mixture will curdle.

Make up $\frac{1}{2}$ lb. glacé icing, tint a little pink
with food colouring, cover cake with remainder. Using No. 1 writing tube, pipe in
parallel lines $\frac{1}{2}$-inch apart while icing is still
wet and "feather" with a skewer first one
way then the other (see p. 18 for various
methods of "feathering").

## MANDARIN MOKA CAKE

(Colour Plate No. 21)

*Make up Sponge Mixture No. 2 (see p. 124), multiplying quantities by 1½ in 2 8 × 12-inch swiss-roll tins.*

Make up a filling as follows:—blend 1½ oz. cornflour with a little milk taken from ¾ pt. Bring rest of milk to the boil, add 4 level teaspoonfuls instant coffee powder and cornflour paste, return to the heat and bring to the boil, stirring continuously. Allow to cool.

Make a cream icing by beating together 5 oz. icing sugar and 5 oz. Superfine Margarine. Add the cornflour mixture to cream icing and beat until light and fluffy. Open 2 11 oz. tins of mandarin oranges, drain well. Reserving at least 20 segments for decorating, chop remaining oranges and fold into about half the cream together with 3 oz. chopped walnuts.

Cut each slab of sponge in two crosswise. Layer the mandarin mixture between the squares of sponge. Cover the top and sides with the remaining cream and decorate with lines of 4 mandarin segments alternating with lines of 4 walnut halves across the top. Arrange on serving dish. (Serves 12.)

**Mandarin Moka Cake: easily cuts up into portions to serve as a party sweet and it looks most impressive before cutting**

Kraft Foods

## DAISY CHAIN CAKE

(Colour Plate No. 21)

*Make up Whisked Sponge Mixture No. 1 (see p. 124) in 2 7-inch sandwich tins.*

Make up ¾ lb. glacé icing. Tint most of it pale yellow with food colouring, reserve a little plain white icing for decorations and keep covered to prevent hardening.

Make a lemon-flavoured butter cream as follows:—beat 2 oz. butter in a mixing bowl until soft and creamy. Add 6 oz. icing sugar a little at a time, beating well after each addition. Add 1½ tablespoonfuls lemon curd and 2 drops yellow food colouring. Use to sandwich the 2 cakes together. Cover the cake with yellow glacé icing and allow to harden.

Divide top into 6 sections, place a tiny sweet (preferably deep yellow or orange in colour) in place for centre of each daisy. Using a small writing tube and white icing, pipe 7 loops for petals round each centre. Tint rest of icing green with food colouring. Using same tube pipe a broken loop of stems between the flowerheads. Place cake on serving plate and tie a pale green ribbon round sides. (If necessary, make template of one broken loop section between 2 daisies, prick out 6 times round top edge of cake.)

**Daisy Chain Cake: delicate colouring and easy but effective icing design on this cake looks just like coloured silk embroidery**

McDougalls Cookery Service

## CHOCOLATE GÂTEAU

(Colour Plate No. 19)

*3 tablespoonfuls honey; 1½ oz. cocoa; 6 oz. margarine;*
*4 oz. soft brown sugar; 1 teaspoonful vanilla essence;*
*3 eggs; 6 oz. s.r. flour.*
  *Decoration: 1 tablespoonful cocoa; 1 lb. 2 oz.*
*butter cream (see recipe p. 19); 2 oz. chopped walnuts;*
*2 oz. plain chocolate; 6 glacé cherries tossed in sugar.*

Line the bases of two 8-inch sandwich tins and grease.

Melt honey, stir in the cocoa and leave to cool. Cream margarine and sugar together, then gradually beat in vanilla essence and eggs, adding a little flour. Stir in honey mixture alternately with the flour. Divide the mixture between the prepared tins. Bake in a moderate oven (electric 350°F., gas mark 4) for about 30 minutes. Turn out and cool on a wire tray.

To decorate the gâteau, dissolve the cocoa in 1 tablespoonful of boiling water and beat into the butter cream. Take out 1 heaped teaspoonful and add a little gravy browning to give a rich dark colour. Place this in a greaseproof paper piping bag with a No. 2 writing tube inserted in the end.

Sandwich the cakes together with a little of the remaining butter cream. Spread the sides of the gâteau with butter cream and roll in chopped walnuts. Spread some more over the top, then pipe lines of the darker butter cream across the top. Draw a skewer alternately up and down, across the lines to give a feather pattern. Pipe 16 rosettes around top edge of the cake with the remaining butter cream and a No. 21 star tube.

To make chocolate triangles, melt chocolate gently over hot water. Spread on waxed paper and leave to set. When set, cut into 1-inch squares, then cut each square into two triangles, using a sharp knife.

To complete the decoration, place six glacé cherries and six chocolate triangles on the rosettes around the top edge of the cake.

## BATTENBURG CAKE

(Colour Plate No. 19)

*6 oz. margarine; 6 oz. castor sugar; 3 eggs; 6 oz. s.r.*
*flour; 1 dessertspoonful cocoa; few drops vanilla*
*essence.*

Line and grease a 7-inch square cake tin, and divide with a piece of folded foil down the centre of the tin.

Cream margarine and sugar together until light and creamy. Beat in the eggs, adding a little of the flour. Fold in remaining flour. Divide the mixture in half; to one half add sieved cocoa and a little milk, and to the other some vanilla essence. Place in the prepared tin and bake in a moderate oven (electric 350°F., gas mark 4) for 25-30 minutes. Turn out and cool.

Trim the cakes, then cut each into two even-sized lengths. Alternating the colours, sandwich the four pieces together with a little raspberry jam. Brush the long outside edges with warmed raspberry jam.

Roll 1 lb. marzipan into a rectangle large enough to cover the cake. Place cake in centre of almond paste and ease to cover the cake. Make sure the join is underneath and well sealed. Trim edges of almond paste. Using a sharp knife mark a diamond design on top of cake and flute the top edges. Decorate with halved glacé cherries and angelica leaves.

**Chocolate Gâteau and Battenburg Cake: chocolate butter cream is used to
fill and decorate the honey-flavoured chocolate gâteau. The Battenburg cake
is easily made by dividing a 7-inch square tin with foil to keep the different
coloured mixtures separate during baking**

Plate 19

Above—Gâteau aux Pêches: tinned peach halves and whipped cream top a sponge

Kraft Foods

Below—Mille Feuilles Gâteau: feather-iced puff pastry filled with jam and custard

Plate 20

**Above — Mandarin Moka Cake:** coffee flavoured creamy filling and coating contrast well with the fresh flavour of mandarin oranges and crisp walnuts, rows of which also decorate the top

Kraft Foods

**Below—Daisy Chain Cake:** just like a piece of dainty embroidery, the decoration of this simple glacé-iced cake is piped on with a fine writing tube in the same style as lazy daisy stitch

McDougalls Cookery Service

Plate 21

A selection of small fancy cakes which are all made from a basic sandwich cake
mixture and decorated in various ways to give a selection which would enhance
any tea-party—see recipes opposite

Plate 22

# Small Cakes

## SMALL CAKES
(Colour Plate No. 22)

**Basic Recipe:** Cream together 4 oz. butter and 4 oz. castor sugar until light and fluffy. Gradually beat in 2 eggs and then lastly fold in 6 oz. sieved s.r. flour.

According to the type of cakes you are making bake in a moderate oven (electric 350°F., gas mark 4) for 12-15 minutes, in paper cake cases, greased patty tins, greased dariole moulds or a swiss roll tin.

**Top Hats** (1): Bake the mixture in paper cake cases. Remove part of the centre of the cake using a small cutter. Fill centre with jam and pipe butter cream on top, using a No. 21 tube. Replace cake centre and dust with icing sugar.

**Butterfly Fancies** (2): Add 1 dessertspoonful cocoa and a little milk to the basic mixture and bake in paper cake cases. Cut off tops of cakes, spread with jam and pipe whipped cream on top, using a No. 21 tube. Split the tops and replace at an angle to represent butterfly wings.

**Jam Jewels** (3): Bake the mixture in paper cake cases. Pipe a border of butter cream stars, using a No. 21 tube, around edge of each cake and fill centres with different coloured jams.

**Flake Cakes** (4): Bake the mixture in paper cake cases. Completely cover the tops of the cakes with butter cream stars, using a No. 21 tube. Cut a chocolate flake bar into 1-inch pieces with a hot sharp knife and place one on top of each cake.

**Iced Cakes** (5): Bake the mixture in paper cake cases. Pipe a circle of butter cream stars, using a No. 21 tube, around edge of each cake and fill centre with pink glacé icing.

**Feather-Iced Cakes** (6): Bake the mixture in paper cake cases. Cover cakes with white glacé icing. Pipe lines of icing, using a No. 2 writing tube, in a contrasting colour across top of icing. Whilst icing is still wet, draw a skewer across in the opposite direction, to obtain a feathered design.

## MADELEINES (7)

*Make up Basic Recipe (see opposite) and place in 18 greased dariole moulds. Bake in a hot oven (electric 425°F., gas mark 7) for 12 minutes.*

Decorate Madeleines by heating 4 tablespoonfuls raspberry jam. Place a fork in the base of the madeleines and brush all over with jam. Roll in 3 oz. desiccated coconut, pressing firmly on to the sides. Pipe a star of butter cream with a No. 21 star tube on top and decorate with glacé cherries and angelica.

To make **owls** (8), substitute 1 oz. cocoa for the same amount of flour from the basic recipe. Continue as above, but decorate with chocolate buttons piped with a butter cream star using a No. 8 tube in the centre for the eyes, and a quarter glacé cherry for the nose.

## ALMOND SLICES (9)

*Make up Basic Recipe (see p. 97) and place in a lined and greased 7-inch square cake tin. Bake in a moderate oven (electric 350°F., gas mark 4) for 30–40 minutes.*

Trim edges of cake, split horizontally and sandwich together with 2 tablespoonfuls apricot jam. Also spread a little over the top. Cut cake in half.

Divide 8 oz. almond paste into three. Colour one third red, one third green, and to the remaining third, knead in some cocoa to colour it brown. Roll each into two 7-inch lengths, and arrange the rolls in a pyramid shape on the centre of each piece of cake. Place on a wire tray.

Break 8 oz. plain chocolate into a saucepan, add 3 tablespoonfuls water and 1 oz. slightly salted butter. Allow to melt over a gentle heat, then beat in 2 oz. sieved icing sugar. Coat the cakes with the chocolate icing. Ensure the slices are completely covered before shaking the wire tray gently to spread the icing evenly. Leave in a cool place to set. Cut into diagonal slices.

## CHOCOLATE BOXES (10)

*Make up Basic Recipe (see p. 97) and place in a lined and greased 11 × 7-inch swiss-roll tin. Bake in a moderate oven (electric 375°F., gas mark 5) for 20 minutes.*

Melt 8 oz. plain chocolate in a basin over hot water. Spread on waxed paper to form a rectangle 12 × 9 inches, and leave to set.

To make syrup, dissolve 4 oz. granulated sugar in ¼ pint water, stirring over a low heat. Boil rapidly for 1 minute, remove from heat and stir in 1 tablespoonful Curaçao or orange squash.

To assemble the chocolate boxes, cut the cake in half across the middle. Sandwich the two halves together with a little strawberry jam. Trim edges. Pour syrup over the

cake allowing it to soak in. Cut cake into 12 1½-inch squares. Brush each square with jam. With a sharp knife cut chocolate into 1½-inch squares and press four around each piece of cake. Cut some into triangles. Using approx. 6 tablespoonfuls of whipped double cream or butter cream, pipe 4 parallel lines on top of each cake, using a No. 21 tube, then decorate with chocolate triangles.

## CHOCOLATE PETITS FOURS

Make up cake base as follows:—Whisk together 4 oz. castor sugar and 4 eggs until thick and frothy. Fold in 2½ oz. sieved flour and 1 level tablespoonful cocoa and 2 oz. melted and cooled margarine. Pour into a shallow

*Cadbury Typhoo Food Advisory Service*

98

tin 12 × 8 inches, and bake in a moderate oven for about 20 minutes. When cold cut into different shapes with sharp knife and round cutter (circles, triangles, rectangles and squares) and decorate similarly as for 4 o'Clock Biscuits, with glacé and butter cream icing.

Either arrange the cakes on a tray and pour glacé icing over to cover them completely or coat top and sides with butter cream, and roll sides in flaked almonds or toasted coconut. Melted chocolate poured onto grease-proof paper can be cut out in tiny heart, leaf

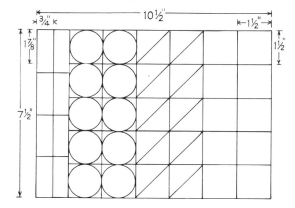

**Trim cake to 7½ × 10 inches, divide as shown in diagram to give 10 squares, 20 triangles, 10 circles and 8 rectangles**

or crescent shapes when set, and used to add finishing touches, or slivers cuts from orange and lemon slices (sweets, not fresh fruit) are effective.

## HOME-MADE CANDIES

**Choc-Rum Truffles:** Melt 6 oz. plain chocolate in a small bowl over saucepan of hot water. Beat until smooth, add 1 egg yolk, 1 oz. Luxury Margarine, 2 teaspoonfuls rum, grated rind 1 orange and 1 teaspoonful milk. Mix thoroughly. Leave until firm in cool place or refrigerator. Mould into small rounds and toss half in chocolate vermicelli and other half in coloured strands. Place in

paper sweet cases, decorate with mimosa balls.

**Peel and Cherry Candy:** Dissolve 8 oz. granulated sugar and ⅛ pt. milk in a saucepan over low heat. Add 1 oz. Luxury Margarine, 1 dessertspoonful golden syrup, continue cooking gently for 2-3 minutes. Add 2 rounded tablespoonfuls condensed milk, boil gently to 240° F. (or to soft ball stage). Stir occasionally to prevent sticking. Remove from heat and stir in 2 oz. mixed peel and 2 oz. chopped glacé cherries. Pour into a 7-inch square tin, previously brushed with Luxury Margarine. Cut into squares with a knife, decorate with half cherries, walnuts or almonds. Leave until set, place in paper sweet cases.

**Coconut Pom-Poms:** Place 1 tablespoonful honey or redcurrant jelly in a small bowl, add 1 oz. Luxury Margarine, and cream together. Add 1 heaped tablespoonful icing sugar, sieved, and beat well. Stir in 4 rounded tablespoonfuls desiccated coconut, until thoroughly mixed. Form into balls and roll into rounds. Then roll in coloured coconut (tint by mixing with a few drops of food colouring in a basin) and leave on wire tray until firm. Place in paper sweet cases and decorate with pieces of glacé cherry.

## CAULIFLOWER CAKES

*Make up Victoria Sponge Mixture No. 2 (see p. 124) in a swiss-roll tin.*

Make up about 1½ lb. Eggless Almond Paste (for recipe see p. 77), and colour pale green with food colouring.

Cut out circles of the sponge with a 1½-inch round cutter. Spread the sides of the sponge circles with lemon curd. Roll out the almond paste and cut circles of paste with the same cutter as used for the sponge. Wrap 4 overlapping circles of paste round each cake, pressing the upper edges open slightly to represent leaves. Whip a 6 oz. tin of Nestlé's pure cream. Using a No. 6 star tube, pipe small stars all over the centres very close together, to represent the flower of the cauliflower.

## PRIMROSE CAKES

*Make up Rich Victoria Sponge Mixture (see p. 124) in a swiss-roll tin.*

Make up about 1½ lb. Eggless Almond Paste (for recipe see p. 77). Using a 3-inch plain cutter, cut out as many rounds of sponge as possible. Brush sides with boiling apricot jam and coat with toasted coconut. Make a small amount of green glacé icing and use to cover in the tops of the cakes.

To make the primrose petals, roll out a little almond paste to ⅛-in. thickness. Using a ½-inch plain cutter, cut 5 small rounds per cake. Pinch the round together at one edge to form a petal. Paint centre with undiluted yellow colouring. Allow to dry for half an hour before using. (Either use extra almond paste for marzipan fruits, or make half quantity only.)

Decorate tops of cakes with 5 petals each and tiny balls of almond paste tinted brown in the centres.

## CHOCOLATE ÉCLAIRS
(Colour Plate No. 4)

**Choux Pastry:** Sieve together 4 oz. Super-Sifted s.r. flour, a pinch of salt and $\frac{1}{2}$ oz. sugar onto a piece of paper. Put $\frac{1}{4}$ pt. water and 2 oz. butter or margarine into a small saucepan, bring to the boil, then add the flour, etc., all at once. Stir quickly with a wooden spoon until the mixture forms a smooth ball of dough. Remove from the heat, add one egg, stir, then beat very thoroughly until it has been absorbed. Repeat with the second egg. Beat the third egg and add sufficient to bring the mixture to a velvety consistency, which will keep its shape when pulled into points with a spoon. Beat thoroughly before use. Put the mixture into a piping bag with a $\frac{5}{8}$-inch plain tube. Pipe 3-inch lengths onto a greased baking sheet about $1\frac{1}{2}$ inches apart, cutting off mixture sharply with a knife. Cook for 30-40 minutes until crisp to the touch, just above the middle of a moderately hot oven. Cool, slit open one side of each éclair. Fill with vanilla or fresh double cream whipped until thick, ice with chocolate glacé icing.

**Vanilla Cream:** Blend 1 rounded teaspoonful cornflour with $\frac{1}{4}$ pt. milk, boil until thick, stirring all the time, leave until cold with a piece of wet paper over the surface to prevent a skin forming. Cream 2 oz. butter or margarine and 2 oz. icing sugar so that the mixture is of the same consistency as the cornflour sauce. Add the latter a spoonful at a time beating well after each addition. Beat in $\frac{1}{4}$ teaspoon vanilla essence and use as directed.

**Chocolate Glacé Icing:** Cut 4 oz. plain chocolate into small pieces, put it and a small knob of butter or margarine into a saucepan with $1\frac{1}{2}$ tablespoonfuls warm water. Stir over gentle heat to a smooth cream. Cool until lukewarm, add 6 oz. sieved icing sugar by degrees, beating thoroughly, and add another spoonful of water if required to bring to a coating consistency. Beat again over gentle heat and test the consistency. Using a

teaspoon, coat the filled éclairs. If the icing becomes too stiff stand the saucepan in a basin of warm water.

## PARTY CHICK CAKES
(Colour Plate No. 3)

*Make up Sponge Mixture No. 2 (see p. 124) in a swiss-roll tin.*

When cool, cut into as many rounds as possible with a $2\frac{1}{2}$-inch plain cutter. Cut each circle in half, using one half for the body of the chick. Cut the head and stand from the remaining half as shown in the diagram below, using a 1-inch cutter for the head.

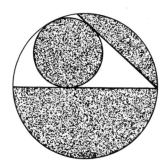

Use a little Pure Apricot Preserves to fasten the body to the stand. Brush stand, body and head with preserves and toss in coarse-cut coconut. Join head to body with preserves. Position currants to represent eyes, and pieces of almonds, halved lengthwise and tinted yellow, for beaks. To colour almonds, soak for 15 minutes in saffron yellow food colouring. Rinse in cold water and dry.

Kraft Foods

## COFFEE BUTTERFLIES

When you are busy, and would like to make some attractive little cakes in a hurry, try this recipe. The extra quick one-stage method soon gives you a plateful of delicious fancy cakes.

You will need 1 ¼ lb. packet Luxury Margarine, 4 oz. s.r. flour, 1 level teaspoonful baking powder, 4 oz. castor sugar, 2 eggs.

Sieve flour and baking powder together into a mixing bowl, add all the other ingredients, quickly mix together, then beat thoroughly with a wooden spoon (press the margarine to the sides of the basin to cream, if refrigerated). Place the mixture in 18 small bun tins, greased with a little margarine. Bake near the top of a fairly hot oven for 15-20 minutes. Cool on a wire tray.

To make the filling, put 2 oz. Luxury Margarine, 1 oz. castor sugar, 1 heaped teaspoonful instant coffee powder and 1 dessertspoonful warm water in a small bowl. Whisk for 1-2 minutes, add 1 dessertspoonful milk a little at a time, then whisk again.

Cut off the tops of the cakes, to make a circle approximately 1½ inches wide, then cut tops in half. Spread a little cream smoothly on top of each cake, and replace the halves in the cream at an angle to form wings. Sieve icing sugar lightly on top. With a small star tube pipe a row of rosettes across tops between the wings.

## CHERRY RIPE CAKES

Make up the same basic one-stage recipe as for Coffee Butterflies, and bake in 18 paper cases, placed in bun tins to help keep their shape. Cool on a wire tray.

Whisk up ¼ pt. of double cream until thick, and with a large star tube pipe a swirl of cream on to the top of each cake, spiralling up to a point. Decorate with a fresh cherry. Other fresh fruits in season, such as strawberries, could be used.

**How to decide if small cakes are cooked**
Use the finger-tip test. Press one cake quickly and lightly with the tip of the forefinger. If resilient and firm, cakes are done, if depression remains, cook for a few minutes more. If possible, raise the position of the tray on which the tins are placed in the oven, or slightly increase the heat during this time.

**Coffee Butterflies: a one-stage recipe makes it easy to prepare these quickly**

**Cherry Ripe Cakes: the same recipe with an entirely different decoration of fruit**

Blue Band Bureau

102

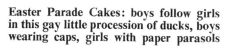

Easter Parade Cakes: boys follow girls in this gay little procession of ducks, boys wearing caps, girls with paper parasols

Chocolate Cream Caps: just cut off the tops, pipe in a swirl of fresh whipped cream or butter cream and replace tops

## EASTER PARADE CAKES

Make up the basic cakes as follows:—cream 4 oz. Table Margarine and 4 oz. castor sugar together until very light. Beat in 2 eggs one at a time, adding a little sieved flour, taken from 4 oz. s.r. flour, with the second. Fold in the remaining flour. Place heaped teaspoonfuls of the mixture in 8 deep bun tins brushed all round inside with melted table margarine, put the remaining mixture in a 7-inch sandwich tin, also brushed inside with melted Table Margarine, and the bottom lined with a round of greaseproof paper. Bake in a moderately hot oven, the buns on the second shelf from the top, for 15-20 minutes, and the sandwich cake on middle shelf for 25 minutes. Turn out and cool on a wire tray.

To make the ducks, trim the buns with scissors, making one side pointed to represent duck "tails". Cut out rounds from the sandwich cake with a 1-inch plain round cutter; trim into ducks' "heads". Add a little yellow colouring to 4 oz. desiccated coconut and rub gently with fingers to make an even yellow colour. Dip the cakes ("heads" and "bodies") in 4 oz. hot sieved apricot jam boiled with 2 tablespoonfuls water, and toss in coconut. Stick "heads" on "bodies" with a little jam. Decorate the cakes to make 4 boy ducks and 4 girl ducks.

Make up 4 oz. almond paste, colour half of it green. Mould the boys' caps, girls' bonnets and scarves from green almond paste. Bonnets can be cut with small fancy round cutter, and mimosa balls placed in centres. The "beaks" are made from paste tinted yellow and the "eyes" from yellow paste with green centres. With brown food colouring draw in sections on caps and pupils of eyes. Place the cakes on a serving plate, the boy ducks following girl ducks, with a paper parasol inserted at one side just below the scarf of each girl duck.

## CHOCOLATE CREAM CAPS

Cream together 3 oz. margarine or butter and 3 oz. castor sugar until light and fluffy. Beat in 1 lightly whisked egg a little at a time and $\frac{1}{2}$ teaspoonful vanilla essence. Fold in 4 oz. s.r. flour and 1 dessertspoonful cocoa sieved together. (Add a little warm water if needed to form a stiff dropping consistency.) Spoon into paper cases arranged on a baking tray or in tart tins. Bake in a fairly hot oven for 10-15 minutes. Allow to cool. Using a sharp knife cut off the top of each cake. Using a large star tube pipe a circle of whipped cream around the cut edge of each cake. Replace the cap.

103

# LITTLE NUNS FROM FRANCE

**Pastry Tartlets:** Put 1 $\frac{1}{4}$ lb. packet Luxury Margarine, 1 level tablespoonful castor sugar, 2 tablespoonfuls taken from 6 oz. plain flour (sieved) and 1 tablespoonful water into a bowl and cream with a fork for about half a minute until well mixed. Stir in remaining flour to form a firm dough. Knead lightly on a floured board. Roll out thinly and cut out rounds with a 3-inch fluted cutter. Line 8-10 patty tins, prick well, line with small pieces of greaseproof paper and fill with baking beans. Bake on second shelf from top of fairly hot oven for 10 minutes. Lift out paper and beans, return to oven for a further 10 minutes. Cool on a wire tray.

**Choux Pastry Puffs:** Put $\frac{1}{4}$ pt. water and 2 oz. Luxury Margarine in a saucepan and bring to the boil over a moderate heat. Remove from heat and stir in 2 oz. plain flour. Return to low heat and beat for 1-2 minutes with a wooden spoon. Remove from heat and add 2 eggs, lightly beaten together, gradually to the mixture, beating very thoroughly until no traces remain. Using a large piping bag and $\frac{1}{2}$-inch plain tube, pipe the mixture into 8-10 large rounds approximately 2$\frac{1}{2}$ inches across and 8-10 small rounds the size of walnuts, onto a baking sheet previously brushed with melted margarine. Bake on the third shelf from top of a hot oven for 15 minutes, then reduce heat to moderately hot for a further 20-25 minutes. Cool on a wire tray.

**Cream Filling:** Bring $\frac{1}{2}$ pt. milk to the boil, beat 3 egg yolks and 6 oz. castor sugar until lemon coloured. Stir in 2 oz. plain flour (sieved), then gradually add the hot milk, stirring. Pour the mixture into a saucepan, bring to the boil and boil for 2-3 minutes, stirring all the time. Remove from the heat and add 1 tablespoonful rum. Divide the cream into approximately $\frac{1}{3}$ and $\frac{2}{3}$. Flavour $\frac{1}{3}$ with 1 heaped teaspoonful instant coffee powder dissolved in 1 teaspoonful hot water; add 2 oz. melted chocolate to the remaining cream. Beat both well and leave to cool.

**Coffee Icing:** Whisk 1 $\frac{1}{4}$ lb. packet Luxury Margarine, 2 oz. castor sugar, 2 heaped teaspoonfuls instant coffee powder and 1 tablespoonful warm water together in a small bowl for 1-2 minutes. Gradually add 1 tablespoonful milk, whisk again until well blended.

**Chocolate Icing:** Put 8 oz. icing sugar, 2 oz. Luxury Margarine and 3 dessertspoonfuls water in a saucepan. Stir over a moderate heat until margarine has melted. Remove from heat and beat well.

**To assemble Little Nuns:** Fill the small puffs with coffee cream and cover with chocolate icing. Fill the larger puffs with chocolate cream. Place a little coffee icing in each tartlet case and put a large puff in the case. Place a small puff on each large one, securing it with a little coffee icing. Place remaining coffee icing in an icing bag with a small rosette tube. Holding bag vertically, pipe rosettes pulling upwards, starting where the small puff joins larger puff. These should look like little flames. Pipe a small rosette in the centre of each top small puff.

## SHAMROCK CAKES

*Make up Whisked Sponge Mixture No. 1 (see p. 124) in 12 greased dariole moulds.*

Trim the bottoms of the cakes so that they stand evenly and are all the same height. When nearly cold, brush them one at a time with melted apricot jam, holding each cake

Cadbury Typhoo Food
Advisory Service

on a skewer, and roll them in desiccated coconut.

Make up 4 oz. almond paste, and tint bright green with food colouring. Roll out very thinly. Make a cardboard template in the shape of a shamrock about 1 inch across. Cut out round this to make 1 "shamrock" for each cake. Make up about 4 oz. butter cream, flavoured with almond essence. Using a large star tube, pipe a big rosette of cream on to each cake. Lay the "shamrocks" at a slight angle on top of the rosettes. Place the cakes in paper cases.

## CHRISTMAS STARS
(Colour Plate No. 4)

Make up basic chocolate cake mixture as follows:—cream together 2 oz. margarine or butter and 2 oz. castor sugar until light and fluffy. Gradually beat in a lightly whisked egg. Fold in 3 oz. s.r. flour and 1 dessertspoonful cocoa, sieved together, adding sufficient warm water to form a dropping consistency. Spoon into greased star-shaped tins. Bake in a moderately hot oven for 10 to 15 minutes. Remove from tins and cool on a wire tray.

Make up about 6 oz. glacé icing of a thick coating consistency. Spread about 1 teaspoonful on the top of each cake, removing any that may run down the sides. When set pipe round edge with stars, using small star tube and butter cream coloured pale green or pink.

Complete the decoration by placing a small holly spray in the centre of each cake.

Brown & Polson

## FLOWER PETAL CAKES

For the basic cake, beat together 3 oz. butter and 3 oz. castor sugar until light and creamy. Beat 2 eggs lightly, add to the creamed mixture alternately with 4 oz. plain flour, 1 oz. cornflour and 1 level teaspoonful baking powder sifted together. Bake in an 8 × 12-inch swiss-roll tin for 20 minutes in a moderate oven.

When cold cut into rounds with a plain 2-inch round cutter. Crumble and sieve 2 stale sponge cakes. Brush sides and tops of the cakes lightly with warmed sieved red jam, roll in the sieved cake crumbs to coat sides. Make up 4 oz. almond paste and tint 3 oz. pink with cochineal, remainder green with food colouring. Roll out thinly. Cut rounds from pink paste with same cutter as for cakes, and press into place on tops. Roll rest of almond paste more thinly still, and cut out tiny circles (for petals) and green leaf shapes.

Decorate tops of some cakes with pink petals, pinched together at centres, and green

leaves, placing mimosa balls in centre of petals. Decorate others with piped sugar flowers, either laid on top of the circle of pink paste and surrounded with leaves, or peeping through slashed centre of the topping of almond paste.

## CHOCOLATE AND RASPBERRY NUT CAKES

**Basic Mix:** Cream together $5\frac{1}{2}$ oz. Superfine Margarine and 11 oz. castor sugar until white and fluffy. Add 2 large eggs and 1 teaspoonful vanilla essence and continue creaming.

**Raspberry Cake:** Sieve together 8 oz. plain flour, $1\frac{1}{4}$ slightly rounded teaspoonfuls baking powder and $\frac{1}{2}$ teaspoonful salt. Fold into half the basic mix, alternately with $\frac{1}{4}$ pt. milk. Bake in an 8-inch square cake tin in a moderate oven for 25-30 minutes. (Make slight dip in centre of mixture.) To make topping, beat $\frac{1}{8}$ pt. double cream until it begins to thicken, add $1\frac{1}{2}$ packets Philadelphia Cream Cheese Spread and continue creaming, fold in 2 tablespoonfuls Pure Pineapple Preserves, spread over top of cooled cake. Sprinkle with chocolate shavings. Cut into squares.

**Chocolate Nut Cake:** Sieve together 6 oz. plain flour, 2 oz. cocoa, $1\frac{1}{4}$ teaspoonfuls baking powder and $\frac{1}{2}$ teaspoonful salt. Fold into rest of basic mix, alternately with $\frac{1}{4}$ pt. milk. Bake as for first mixture. To make topping, use $\frac{1}{8}$ pt. double cream, $1\frac{1}{2}$ packets Phila-

Kraft Foods

106

delphia Cream Cheese Spread and 2 table-spoonfuls Pure Red Raspberry Preserves, as for topping for first cake. Sprinkle top with 2 oz. chopped walnuts. Cut cake into squares.

## EASTER BONNET BISCUITS

**Bonnet Brims:** Beat 3 oz. butter and 3 oz. sugar together until light and creamy. Sift together 6 oz. flour, 2 oz. cornflour and 1 level teaspoonful baking powder, add to the creamed mixture alternately with one beaten egg. Knead lightly to make a smooth, firm dough and roll out thinly. Cut into rounds with a 3-inch biscuit cutter, making some plain and others with fluted edges. Bake some biscuits flat on a baking tin and others on inverted patty tins, to make a curved "brim". Bake in a moderate oven for 20 minutes.

**Bonnet Crowns:** Slice marshmallows in half and put one in the centre of each biscuit for the crown. Cover each "hat" with glacé icing tinted in various pastel colours and suitably flavoured. A variety of coloured and flavoured icings can be very simply made by using flavoured cornflour with icing sugar, in the proportions of 1 teaspoonful flavoured cornflour to 8 oz. icing sugar. For the best results the icing should be fairly stiff. When the icing is firm, trim the hats in various ways. Using a small writing tube, pipe a "ribbon" round the base of the crown. Add piped sugar flowers, marzipan leaves, even

Spry Cookery Service

tiny feathers or artificial holly berries. (Remember to remove these before eating.)

## EASTER TREAT BUNS

**Bun Mixture:** Put 2 oz. Spry, 2 oz. soft brown sugar, 3 oz. s.r. flour, 1 rounded teaspoonful mixed spice, a pinch of salt, 1 egg, 4 oz. mixed dried fruit, 1 oz. chopped glacé cherries and 1 oz. chopped walnuts all into a mixing bowl. Using a wooden spoon, beat for about 1 minute until well mixed. (Beating will not make the mixture heavy.) Divide mixture into 12 bun tins, brushed with melted Spry. Smooth tops with a knife. Bake near top of a moderately hot oven for 15-20 minutes. Cool on a wire cake rack.

**Decorations:** Brush bun tops with hot apricot jam. Knead 1 lb. almond paste until soft and pliable. Take a small piece and roll into a sausage shape long enough to fit round the top of each bun as a border. Bake near top of a hot oven for 2-3 minutes, until paste is lightly browned. Fill the centres with glacé icing. Make some of the buns into "nests" with chocolate coconut and eggs moulded from some of the remaining paste, tinted various colours and painted with tiny dots of brown food colouring. Finish the others with rabbits or chicks moulded from rest of al-

Brown & Polson

mond paste. Ears are made from toasted almonds, eyes and nose from silver balls. Hats or caps are shaped round the heads from tiny circles of very thin paste.

## AFTERNOON TEA PASTRIES
(Colour Plate No. 6)

### Cream Crisps

Make up 8 oz. puff pastry and chill. Roll out the pastry $\frac{1}{4}$-inch thick into a square as large as possible. Roll up like a swiss roll and chill again. Cut down in slices $\frac{1}{2}$-inch wide with a hot, wet knife. Place each piece on a wet baking sheet. Bake in a hot oven till golden brown (about 8-10 minutes). Remove from tray and leave to cool.

Spread half the layers with Nestlé's Cream, taken from a 6 oz. tin. Sandwich together with the remaining layers, slightly at an angle, piping in 6 large rosettes of cream roughly $\frac{2}{3}$ of the way round edge with a large star tube, and alternating the rosettes with 4 glacé cherries. Dust with icing sugar.

### Cream Slices

Make up 8 oz. puff pastry, roll out thinly and evenly into a large square or oblong, a little larger than baking sheet. Lift carefully on to wet sheet and trim edges with sharp knife. Prick well all over. Chill for 30 minutes. Bake in a hot oven until crisp and firm (about 8-10 minutes). Remove from baking sheet and cool. Using a sharp knife, cut into three even-sized pieces.

Spread one piece of pastry with jam and Nestlé's Cream, cover with another piece of pastry and again spread on jam and cream. (any red jam is suitable.) Top with the third piece of pastry. Dust with sieved icing sugar. With a sharp knife cut into neat pieces.

### Cream Horns

Make up 8 oz. puff pastry. Roll out pastry $\frac{1}{4}$-inch thick. Cut into strips $\frac{1}{2}$-inch wide by 12 inches long and wind round cream horn tins, overlapping slightly. Place on a wet baking sheet and chill for 30 minutes. Bake in

a hot oven till golden brown (8-10 minutes.) Remove from horn cases. Cool, and fill to within $\frac{1}{2}$-inch of top with raspberry jam.

With a large star tube pipe extra large rosettes on top, moving tube round in spirals and finally pulling up to a point on top.

### Meringues

Make the meringue cases by placing 2 egg whites into a perfectly clean and dry bowl, with a pinch of cream of tartar. Whisk to a stiff point. Add 2 oz. castor sugar and whisk again. Fold in another 2 oz. sugar, divide into smaller bowls and fold in various food colourings with a metal spoon.

Have ready a double sheet of greaseproof paper brushed with olive oil. Place this on a baking sheet or board. Using a piping bag and large star tube, pipe meringues on to the paper, drawing up to a sharp point. Dredge lightly with castor sugar and dry off in a cool oven until firm and dry. If making large meringues, turn them over when firm, leave them upside down to dry out. Do not let oven get hot enough to colour meringues or they will be spoilt.

When cool sandwich together with a little Nestlé's Cream taken from a 6-oz. tin, and use a small star tube to pipe small rosettes round the joins.

## CHOCOLATE BOATS

Cream together 2 oz. butter and 2 oz. castor sugar until light and fluffy, and gradually beat in one lightly whisked egg. Stir in 2 oz. ground almonds. Fold in 3 oz. s.r. flour sieved with 1 dessertspoonful cocoa. Add sufficient warm water to form a soft dropping consistency. Spoon into greased boat-shaped tins. Bake in a moderate oven for 10-15 minutes. Cool on a wire tray.

Make up 6 oz. chocolate butter cream, and beat in 1 tablespoon of rum, or a few drops of rum essence. Coat tops of cakes with this and sprinkle them with split almonds.

Novelty Shape Biscuits: let your little girl follow this recipe herself to make and decorate a batch of crisp, fancy biscuits

## NOVELTY SHAPE BISCUITS

Children love making their own sweets, so why not give your little girl an even more rewarding introduction to cookery—these simple biscuits, which with the aid of fancy cutters, give a really professional looking result. Let her follow the recipe.

1. Get together the kitchen scales, 1 large basin, 1 small basin, 1 egg whisk, 1 dessertspoon, 1 rolling pin, 1 palette knife, 1 baking tray (greased with a piece of buttery paper), a wire cake tray, cutters in different shapes such as circles, stars, animals.

2. Measure out 4 oz. s.r. flour and 1 oz. sugar into the big basin together with a pinch of salt and 2 oz. butter or margarine. Rub together with the fingertips until no more lumps of fat are left in the flour.

3. Add flavouring—work in 2 spoonfuls of coconut if you want coconut biscuits, or 1 spoonful of drinking chocolate powder and 1 drop of vanilla essence if you want chocolate biscuits.

4. Break an egg into the small basin and beat up with the whisk. Take 2 spoonfuls of the egg, add to the flour and stir until it forms one lump, firm but not sticky. Add more egg if needed. Sprinkle flour onto the rolling pin and table or pastry board. Roll out lump of dough until it is thin.

5. Take your cutters and cut out all the shapes, using one round cutter inside a larger one for rings, and put onto greased tray as you cut them. Gather up the bits, pat them together, roll out and make more biscuits. Put the baking tray in the middle of a moderate oven (ask Mummy to adjust heat) and cook for about 12 minutes. Take out, using an oven cloth, and transfer to wire tray to cool.

6. Make up butter cream by creaming 4 oz. butter and gradually adding 6 oz. sifted icing sugar. Add sufficient cocoa to half the butter cream to make chocolate coloured. Either spread all over the biscuits, or use a syringe and small writing tube and pipe all round the edges. Decorate with silver balls, small sweets, quartered glacé cherries. Look at the picture of finished biscuits closely to see how it is done.

Fancy cutters make it simpler to get shapes you can easily outline or cover all over with a soft butter cream icing

Flour Advisory Bureau

Brown & Polson

# International

From the oblong cake cut 3 rounds, 2, 3 and 4 inches in diameter. Then using the 7-inch sponge as a base, build up a pyramid of sponge rings, sandwiching them together with a little butter cream and apricot jam. Spread more butter cream round the edges of each layer and press the meringues round the outside, filling in with rosettes of the cream, using a No. 8 star tube. Fix a silver ball to the tip of each meringue with butter cream.

## USING NON-STICK PARCHMENT

Siliconised parchment can be used to line baking sheets and cake tins to prevent meringues, macaroons and other cakes from sticking. Bakewell, this form of completely non-stick siliconised parchment, is available from stationers and some grocers and supermarkets.

## BAVARIAN COFFEE TORTE
(Colour Plate No. 5)

**Basic Cake:** Sift together 6 oz. plain flour, 2 level teaspoonfuls baking powder, ½ level teaspoonful salt into a mixing bowl, add 5 oz. soft brown sugar. Whisk together the yolks of 2 eggs, 6 tablespoonfuls corn oil, and 2 tablespoonfuls coffee essence made up to 6 tablespoonfuls with milk. Add to the dry ingredients. Beat well to form a smooth slack batter. Fold in the stiffly beaten egg whites. Turn the mixture into an 8-inch cake tin, greased and bottom-lined with greaseproof paper. Bake for about 40 minutes in a moderate oven. Turn out and leave to get cold.

**Coffee Syrup Topping:** Boil 4 oz. sugar and ¼ pt. strong black coffee briskly together for 5 minutes. Remove from the heat and stir in

## MERINGUE PYRAMID

Prepare 3 round sandwich tins, approximately 5, 6 and 7 inches in diameter, and 1 oblong tin 7×11 inches, by greasing lightly. Beat together 12 oz. butter and 12 oz. castor sugar until white and creamy. Sift together 12 oz. flour, 4 oz. cornflour and 4 level teaspoonfuls baking powder. Add to the creamed mixture alternately with 6 beaten eggs. Add a little milk if necessary to give a soft dropping consistency, turn into the prepared tins. Bake for 20-25 minutes in a moderate oven.

**Meringues:** Separate 3 eggs, beat the whites stiffly with a pinch of salt. Add 3 oz. castor sugar and beat again till the mixture stands in peaks. Sift 1 oz. cornflour with another 3 oz. castor sugar and fold into the beaten egg whites. Cover a baking tray with greased greaseproof paper and using a large piping bag and small plain tube, pipe the meringue into small pointed domes, about 1 inch across. Dry off in a very cool oven.

**To assemble the cake:** Make up 1 lb. butter cream, flavoured with rum or rum essence.

# Cake Section

2 tablespoonfuls brandy. When the cake is cold, return to the tin. Pour the hot syrup over and leave overnight. Turn the cake out on to a board.

**Decorations:** Whip $\frac{1}{4}$ pt. cream fairly stiff, and spread a thin layer round the sides of the cake. Chop 1 oz. almonds and 1 oz. hazel nuts finely, and roll the cake in these to coat the sides. Stand cake on serving dish. Fill rest of cream into piping bag with large star tube and pipe parallel lines about 1 inch apart across the top in both directions. Pipe a shell border with the same tube. Finish border with an inner ring of quartered red glacé cherries, and an outer ring of green glacé cherries placed between the red ones.

## VIENNESE MOCCA CAKE

*Make up Coffee Cake Mixture (see p. 125) in an 8-inch round tin.*

When cold split the cake and sandwich together with a layer of coffee butter icing (using 6 oz. icing sugar, 3 oz. butter and 2 table-spoonfuls strong black coffee). Coat sides with a thin layer of butter icing, then roll in fine cake crumbs mixed with a few grated nuts. Reserve enough icing for decoration.

Ice top of cake with coffee glacé icing, reserving enough for piping decorations. To get a smooth shiny finish, pour the warm icing in the centre of the top of cake in a steady stream, allowing it to find its own level, tilting the cake if necessary. If it does not quite reach edge evenly this will be covered by the wide piped border.

To pipe the word "MOCCA" with an elaborate flourish at the end, stiffen the icing with a little more sugar. Prick out outline of word and flourish with a fine skewer when top is dry, and outline this with a fine writing tube, and part of the icing coloured and

Coffee Information Bureau

flavoured chocolate with the addition of a little cocoa powder. Using the coffee icing and small ribbon tube No. 30, fill in the letters and the flourish.

Now put the rest of the butter icing in a forcing bag with a No. 21 star tube, and pipe large, elongated shells round the edge of the cake, doubling the first part of the shell and drawing the tube out to a long point. Place a chocolate button at each of these points.

## KENTUCKY NUT CAKE
(Colour Plate No. 5)

Grease two 7-inch sandwich tins. Cream together 4 oz. margarine and 4 oz. soft brown sugar. Beat in 2 eggs. Add $\frac{1}{4}$ pt. milk and 1 tablespoonful thick honey. Stir in 2 oz. chopped walnuts, 8 oz. s.r. flour, $\frac{1}{2}$ level teaspoonful salt and 1 dessertspoon-ful cocoa. Divide mixture into the prepared tins. Bake in a moderate oven (electric 350° F., gas mark 4) for 25-30 minutes. When cold sandwich together with half the butter cream, made as follows: cream together 4 oz. butter and 8 oz. icing sugar with a little vanilla essence to make a soft cream. Cover the top with remaining butter cream and mark in wavy lines with a fork; place milk chocolate buttons overlapping around the edge.

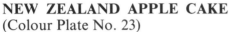

## NEW ZEALAND APPLE CAKE
(Colour Plate No. 23)

**Basic Apple-Fruit Cake:** Cream together 8 oz. butter and 8 oz. soft brown sugar until light and fluffy, and then gradually beat in the grated rind of 1 lemon, $\frac{1}{4}$ pint unsweetened thick apple purée, and 3 eggs; add a little flour (taken from 12 oz. plain flour) to prevent curdling. Sift together rest of flour, $\frac{1}{2}$ level teaspoon bicarbonate of soda, 1 level teaspoonful powdered cinnamon, 1 level teaspoonful ground ginger, 1 level teaspoonful mixed spices. Fold the rest of the flour and spices into the mixture. Stir in 6 oz. sultanas, 6 oz. seedless raisins, 6 oz. currants, 2 oz. mixed peel, and 2 oz. roughly chopped walnuts. Turn the mixture into a greased and lined 8-inch round cake tin, tie some brown paper round the outside and bake in a slow oven for 2-3 hours. Leave to cool in the tin. (The cake is done when a fine skewer comes out clean, and no sizzling noise can be heard.)

**Almond Paste:** Make up a stiff almond paste with 8 oz. ground almonds, 8 oz. sifted icing sugar, 1 teaspoonful lemon juice and 2 egg yolks. (Reserve 1 white for the frosting.) Reserve some paste to form apple decorations and roll out the rest into a circle to cover the top of the cake. Brush top with sieved apricot jam and press the almond paste on to it. Roll flat with a rolling pin. Make up $\frac{1}{2}$ lb. icing sugar with the reserved egg white for a stiff frosting. Spread over the top of the cake and when nearly set, fork into a rough surface.

**Decorations:** Roll about $\frac{2}{3}$ of the rest of the almond paste into about 8 balls for the apples. Press a dent with the forefinger into the top of each and stick in a clove to form a stalk. Paint with diluted cochineal or pink food colouring. Work sufficient green food colouring into remaining paste to tint pale green. Roll out, cut into pointed leaves. Score veins with back of table knife, and paint with undiluted green food colouring. Arrange ring of apples on top of cake alternately with leaves, and place on serving plate with any apples and leaves left over arranged round the base.

**Right—Lemon Snow-Frosted Cake:** an American favourite, snowy Angel Cake baked in a ring tin, filled with lemon butter cream and coated with yellow Snow Frosting

Davis Gelatine

**Right—New Zealand Apple Cake:** the rich, moist fruit mixture includes apple purée for the basic cake. The top has a soft frosting ringed with marzipan apples

Fruit Producers' Council

Plate 23

**Above—Tropical Banana Cake:**
bananas are baked into the cake
and the fudge frosting is decorated with a spider's web design
and moulded marzipan bananas

Banana Co-operative Campaign

**Left—S. African Peach Gâteau:**
a rectangular cake simply made
by slicing a swiss-roll shape in
half lengthwise, topped by fresh
peach halves and grapes, and
piped swirls of fresh cream

Deciduous Fruit Board

Plate 24

## TROPICAL BANANA CAKE
(Colour Plate No. 24)

**Banana Fudge Layers:** Grease 2 7-inch sandwich tins and cut circles of greaseproof paper to fit the bottoms. Grease these papers *heavily* using about 1 oz. butter for the two. Spread with demerara sugar, dividing 3 oz. between them, and arrange 2 bananas sliced in rings on top of each. Make up a cake mixture by creaming 4 oz. butter or margarine with 4 oz. castor sugar, whisk together 2 eggs and 2-3 drops vanilla essence and gradually beat in the whisked egg and vanilla mixture. Add 6 oz. sifted s.r. flour, half at a time, folding it in lightly and adding 2-3 tablespoonfuls milk as required to produce a medium soft dropping consistency. Spread over the banana mixture in the prepared tins. Bake in a moderately hot oven until firm (25-30 minutes). Cool on wire cake tray.
**Coffee Filling and Fudge Icing:** While the cake is cooling, prepare the filling by beating together 2 oz. unsalted butter or margarine, 3 oz. sifted icing sugar and 1-2 teaspoonfuls coffee essence. Sandwich the 2 sponges together, banana layers inside, with the coffee filling. To make the icing, sift 7 oz. icing sugar into a bowl. Put 1 level tablespoonful golden syrup, 2 dessertspoonfuls milk, 1½ oz. margarine sliced up, and 2 teaspoonfuls coffee essence (or to taste) in a saucepan and stir over a gentle heat until the fat is melted, but without allowing the mixture to boil. Pour into the icing sugar and stir until smooth. Leave to cool slightly, stirring from time to time, and when thick enough to leave a good trail, the icing is ready to use. Spread the icing over the cake and make a series of sweeping swirls by passing the tip of a table knife from side to side over the top of the cake.

**Decorating:** To make the shell design, draw the tip of a skewer right down the centre of the iced cake whilst the icing is still soft. Draw similar lines one inch on either side of the centre line, drawing the lines all down to one point on the opposite side of the cake. Continue to draw slanting lines on either side of the cake until the shell design is complete. Cover the sides with remaining coffee fudge icing. Model and colour small bananas from almond paste (see p. 32) and arrange 5 or 6 bananas at the point of the shell design in a "hand".

Banana Co-operative Campaign

## SOUTH AFRICAN PEACH GÂTEAU
(Colour Plate No. 24)

**Basic Sponge:** Grease and line a swiss-roll tin. Whisk together 3 eggs and 4 oz. castor sugar over hot water until thick. Remove from heat and whisk until cool and thick enough to leave a trail. Sift in $3\frac{1}{2}$ oz. s.r. flour, and begin to fold in very lightly, cutting it in with the edge of a metal spoon. When the flour is half mixed in trickle in 3 tablespoonfuls corn oil or $1\frac{1}{2}$ oz. melted butter, and continue to fold in very lightly until evenly mixed. Spread in the prepared tin and bake in a moderately hot oven until firm (about 12-20 minutes). Turn on to a wire tray to cool. When cold cut in half lengthwise and sandwich the two strips together with peach jam.

**Glazed Peach Decoration:** Make up an apricot glaze as follows. Dissolve 2 oz. castor sugar in 2 tablespoonfuls water and 1 tablespoonful lemon juice. Add 3 heaped tablespoonfuls apricot jam. Heat until almost boiling then strain into a clean pan. Re-boil and continue to cook gently until glaze hangs in syrupy drops from spoon. Cool to a good coating consistency before using. Spread a thin layer of apricot glaze on top of the cake. On top of this arrange fresh peach halves (skinned, stoned and blanched by boiling for 3-4 minutes in a medium sugar syrup made with 4 oz. sugar to $\frac{1}{4}$ pt. water). Coat the peaches generously with apricot glaze and leave to set. Spread a thin layer of glaze on the sides of the cake and coat with flaked, toasted almonds.

**Piped Decorations:** Make up a butter cream by beating together 3 oz. unsalted butter and 3 oz. sifted icing sugar. Add a few drops of vanilla essence. Using a savoy bag and large star tube, pipe a looped border of butter cream down both sides of the cake. Garnish the peaches with a rosette of butter cream topped with half a black grape. (If preferred use whipped fresh cream for piping, as the flavour goes well with fresh fruit.)

**Deciduous Fruit Board**

114

## LEMON SNOW-FROSTED CAKE
(Colour Plate No. 23)

*Make up an Angel Cake (see p. 90) in a 7-inch tube tin.*

Make up lemon butter cream filling as follow:—beat 6 oz. icing sugar and 4 oz. butter together until light and smooth and gradually beat in the strained juice of ½ lemon. Split cake through the centre, and sandwich together with lemon butter cream.

Make up American Snow Frosting as follows:—dissolve 1 level teaspoonful gelatine in 3 tablespoonfuls hot water. Bring 8 tablespoonfuls water to the boil in a strong saucepan, add 6 oz. granulated sugar. Stir until sugar dissolves, then boil steadily until the syrup forms a thread when dropped from the spoon. (If using a sugar thermometer, until it registers 240° F.) Brush down the sides of the saucepan with a brush dipped in cold water during this time, but do not stir the syrup. Pour in the gelatine, remove from heat at once, and mix well. Pour the mixture slowly onto 2 stiffly beaten egg whites, beating with the spoon, and add a few drops of yellow food colouring and if liked ½ teaspoon lemon essence. Now beat thoroughly, if possible with a rotary hand beater or electric mixer, until mixture is thick enough to hold its shape. Place cake on a wire tray and pour over the frosting. Spread gently with a knife blade to coat the cake evenly. Leave several hours to set, when the icing will be smooth and glossy. Divide top into 6 equal sections, and in each place a piece of crystallised violet, flanked with diamond-shaped wings of angelica.

Many variations can be achieved with this basic frosting. For instance, fill the cake with a layer of coffee butter cream, and dissolve the gelatine in hot black coffee instead of water. (Omit lemon essence and yellow food colouring.) Mix chopped walnuts with the butter cream, and use half walnuts to decorate the top of the cake.

Davis Gelatine

**Continental Chocolate Gâteau: an attractive gâteau, based on a Victoria Sandwich Cake Mixture, sandwiched together and piped with butter cream; the chocolate triangles are cut from run-out chocolate**

## CONTINENTAL CHOCOLATE GÂTEAU

*Make up Chocolate Victoria Sandwich Mixture (see p. 126) in 2 7-inch sandwich tins.*

Make up about ¾ lb. butter cream and flavour to taste with rum essence or with rum. Split each cake in half and make up a 4-layer sandwich cake with thin layers of rum-flavoured butter cream. Spread a little cream thinly round the sides and roll the sides in chocolate vermicelli. Press to coat evenly by rolling a jam jar round the sides. Spread a thin layer of butter cream over the top of the cake.

With a No. 14 star tube pipe rosettes all over the top of the cake. Pipe a large coiled rosette in the centre, building up several layers, and top with a sugar flower and tiny fronds of maidenhair fern.

Melt 2 oz. plain chocolate in a bowl over pan of hot water. Spread chocolate on to

waxed paper to form a square 6 inches by 3 inches. When set, cut six strips 3 inches long and 1 inch wide. Cut each strip in half to form two triangles and use to decorate gâteau as shown in picture.

## AMERICAN APRICOT DINNER CAKE

**Basic Cake:** Cream 6 oz. butter, 6 oz. castor sugar and 3 drops vanilla essence until light and fluffy. Beat in 3 medium eggs, one at a time, adding a tablespoonful of flour taken from 8 oz. s.r. flour with each. Fold in rest of flour alternately with 3 tablespoonfuls milk. Turn into well greased 8-inch ring tin. Bake in centre of oven at very moderate heat for 1 hour. Turn out and cool on a wire tray.

**Vanilla Cream:** Cream 6 oz. butter or margarine until light and fluffy with 12 oz. icing sugar, beat in 1 tablespoonful milk, 4 drops vanilla essence and 2 drops almond essence only. Cut cake in half horizontally and sandwich together with a thick layer of the cream, mixed with 4-5 apricot halves, drained and coarsely chopped. Spread top and sides of cake with remaining cream, smoothing with blade of a knife round sides and in concentric circles on top of cake. Decorate top of cake with pairs of toasted almonds, placed together at an angle like butterfly wings. Serve portions of the cake with bowls of tinned apricots as a dessert.

## AMERICAN DEVIL'S FOOD

**Basic Cake:** Grease 4 8-inch sandwich tins and line the bottoms with greaseproof paper. Sieve 12 oz. plain flour, 12 oz. castor sugar, 3 oz. cocoa, $\frac{1}{4}$ level teaspoon bicarbonate of soda, $1\frac{1}{2}$ level teaspoonfuls baking powder and $\frac{1}{2}$ level teaspoon salt into a mixing bowl. Whisk together 12 fl. oz. sour milk, 6 fl. oz. corn oil and 1 teaspoonful vanilla essence, and add to the dry ingredients. Beat well to form a smooth, slack mixture and divide between the prepared tins. Bake 25-30 minutes in a moderately hot oven. Turn out and leave to cool. When cold sandwich together with whipped double cream.

Cover with Swirled Marshmallow Frosting (see recipe on p. 92).

## AUSTRALIAN BARINYA CAKE

**Basic Cake:** Cream 4 oz. Australian butter and 6 oz. castor sugar together. Beat in 2 eggs gradually, sift 8 oz. s.r. flour and a pinch of salt together and fold in to mixture alternately with 3 tablespoonfuls milk. Fold in the pulp from 2 passion fruit (known here as grenadillas and in season from October to December) and 1 mashed banana. Turn into a greased 7-inch round tin, lined on the bottom with greaseproof paper and bake in a moderate oven for 45-50 minutes. Turn cake onto wire tray and cool.

Boil the passion fruit skins in a little water for a few minutes and use some of this liquid to make the icing, which will be pale pink and flavoured with passion fruit. Use enough liquid blended with 8 oz. sieved icing sugar to give a good coating consistency. Pour over cake. Decorate with thin slices of tinned pears, well drained, halved glacé cherries and strips of angelica. Score sides of cake into 9 portions, from the tip of each pear slice down sides to base.

Above—American Devil's Food: has a filling of whipped cream and Marshmallow Frosting

Pascall Marshmallows

Left—American Apricot Dinner Cake: fruit-filled ring cake to serve with bowls of apricots

Right—Australian Barinya Cake: try it when fresh passion fruit are in season here

Australian Dairy Produce Board

## HOW TO FREEZE CAKES

Cakes are among the best candidates for the freezer I know. It is a boon to be able to complete a decorated cake in advance when one is not busy and store it safely and freshly until required. Another time-saver is to make a quantity of sponge layers or cup cakes ready to fill and decorate, and freeze these for future use.

### Freezing uncooked cake mixtures

Start with a basic sandwich mixture, made in quantity. Measure into containers each holding just enough for a 7-inch layer (the Tupperware Cereal Bowl takes exactly the right amount). Defrost and shake vigorously before unsealing, turn each one into a prepared tin and bake off. Fruit cake mixture can be made up at a convenient time and stored uncooked in the same way until you have an opportunity to bake cakes. With large quantities, the centre of the mixture must be fully defrosted when you put it in the tin.

You may prefer to make up a number of sandwich layers, and defrost two or three at a time for a fancy gâteau. Put dividers between the layers, or they may stick together. A length of foil or greaseproof paper folded several times to make a wide "ruler" shape can be pressed down the side of the container, across the bottom and up the other side, leaving two protruding ends long enough to grasp, tucked under the seal. These ends can be used to bring a pile of layers or a finished cake up and out easily, without inverting the container.

Fully decorated cakes need careful handling to freeze without damage. Open freeze on a baking sheet, or on a seal. In the first case transfer to the container when quite hard, and seal. If you place the cake to freeze *on* the seal, invert the container on top and press into place. Label the container on the bottom so that you do not inadvertently turn it upside down later, but take care the seal is perfect and it will stand the weight of the cake. Or put the frozen cake in a large gussetted polythene bag, lightly fix the twist tie and draw out all the surplus air through a straw. Seal firmly as you withdraw the straw. Always place cakes for freezing on a board, or if possible on the plate from which they will be served. Small fancy cakes are so easily damaged even when fully frozen that it pays to take extra care in packing them. A large, fairly flat container should be used, the base filled with one layer of cakes. Open freeze, and when hard, cover lightly with a layer of foil, but do not press it down. Arrange another layer of cakes on top, well clearing the seal, which can then be snapped on. Keep quite level in the freezer until fully frozen. Fortunately each layer takes only about 2 hours to freeze.

### Defrosting cakes successfully

To defrost, remove any covering while cakes are still hard and unlikely to be damaged. Do not leave until the icing is soft enough to stick to the covering surface. During the thawing process, moisture is also likely to form inside a bag or closed container and spoil the surface, especially if cakes are decorated with melted chocolate.

Fruit cakes can be stored in the freezer but are better in airtight tins from the point of view of maturing. Freezing halts maturing. Iced cakes, such as a wedding tier saved for a christening, keep well, but are liable to defrost with dark patches where the oil from the almond paste has discoloured the icing and shows through. This is not a tragedy, as the decoration can be carefully chipped off and the cake given a thin extra coating of icing before re-decorating. My favourite recipes for the cake itself if intended for freezing are those using oil because there is no danger of rancidity during long storage. When defrosted, the feather sponge is very moist and the same applies to a fruit cake made with oil.

# Basic Cake Recipes

## EGGLESS FRUIT CAKE MIXTURE

*1 oz. glacé cherries; 2 oz. chopped almonds; ¼ pt. water; 5 oz. margarine; 4 oz. currants; 4 oz. sultanas; 2 oz. mixed peel; rind of ½ lemon and ½ orange, grated; 7 tablespoonfuls Nestlé's Condensed Milk; 5 oz. flour; pinch of salt; ½ level tablespoonful bicarbonate of soda.*

Chop cherries and place in a saucepan with water, margarine, fruit, grated rinds and condensed milk. Bring to boil and boil for 3 minutes. Allow to cool. Add the bicarbonate of soda to this and then the sieved flour. Place in a prepared cake tin as directed on p. 77 for the Sack Cake. Bake in a slow oven (electric 325° F., gas mark 2) on the middle shelf, for 1½ hours. For the Choir Boy Cake (see p. 79) double the quantities and bake in 2 containers as directed in a slow oven, 2¾ hours for the large cake and 1 hour for the small one.

## SIMNEL WREATH CAKE

*7 oz. flour; 1 oz. cornflour; 6 oz. butter; 6 oz. castor sugar; grated rind ½ lemon; 1 oz. ground almonds; 1 level teaspoonful mixed spice; 3 eggs; 1 tablespoonful brandy; ¾ lb. currants; 2 oz. chopped candied peel.*

Beat the butter and sugar together until white and creamy, add the lemon rind and ground almonds and continue beating. Sift the flour, cornflour and spice together. Add to the creamed mixture alternately with the beaten eggs and brandy. Add the currants and chopped peel. Continue as directed, in the recipe on p. 81.

## TRADITIONAL SIMNEL CAKE

*8 oz. super-sifted s.r. flour; ¼ teaspoonful salt; ½ teaspoonful mixed spice; 4 oz. butter or margarine; 4 oz. soft brown sugar; 8 oz. currants; 8 oz. sultanas; 4 oz. glacé cherries; 4 oz. mixed cut peel;*

*3 eggs; ½ teaspoonful gravy browning; 5 tablespoonfuls milk.*

Sieve together the flour, salt and spices into a bowl. Add the fat cut into small pieces. Rub in to the dry ingredients until it resembles fine breadcrumbs. Stir in the sugar and fruit. Mix the eggs, milk and gravy browning well together. Make a well in the centre of the dry ingredients and add the eggs etc., and mix thoroughly. Continue as directed, in the recipe on p. 73.

## CHRISTMAS CAKE MIXTURE

*6 oz. superfine margarine; 6 oz. soft brown sugar; 1 oz. ground almonds; 4 eggs; juice and rind of ½ lemon; 8 oz. flour; 1½ level teaspoonfuls mixed spice, sieved together; 9 oz. currants; 8 oz. sultanas; 2 oz. mixed peel; 4 oz. glacé cherries, chopped.*

Prepare the fruit on the day before baking. Soak currants and sultanas separately to loosen grit. Wash well, drain, dry and spread on oven tray. Dry for 2-3 hours at electric 200° F., at gas mark ¼. (NOTE: Wet fruit sinks to the bottom of the cake.) Prepare and line an 8-inch cake tin. Cream the margarine and sugar until light and fluffy. Add ground almonds and beat in well. Add the lightly whisked eggs, 2 tablespoonfuls at a time, and beat in thoroughly before next addition. Repeat until ¼ of the egg quantity is added and then add 2 tablespoonfuls of the sieved flour mixture. Add remaining egg as before, beat in thoroughly and add lemon juice. Fold in (do not beat) another 2 tablespoonfuls of the flour mixture. Add currants, sultanas, cherries, peel and rind. Fold in remaining flour thoroughly. Transfer the mixture, now of a stiff dropping consistency, to the prepared tin and bake at electric 300° F., gas mark 2, for 2 hours. Reduce heat to 275° F., gas mark 1, for further 2½-3 hours.

**FRUIT CAKE MIXTURE No. 1**

The quantities required are given for 6-inch, 8-inch and 11-inch round tins, or for 5-inch, 7-inch and 10-inch square tins, but the method in all cases is the same.

NOTE: For example, square 5-inch tin requires same amount of mixture as 6-inch round tin.

| *6-inch round or 5-inch square tin* | *8-inch round or 7-inch square tin* | *11-inch round or 10-inch square tin* |
|---|---|---|
| *4 oz. super sifted s.r. flour* | *7 oz. super sifted s.r. flour* | *16 oz. super sifted s.r. flour* |
| *⅛ teaspoonful mixed spice* | *¼ teaspoonful mixed spice* | *½ teaspoonful mixed spice* |
| *pinch of salt* | *good pinch of salt* | *¼ teaspoonful salt* |
| *3 oz. soft brown sugar* | *5 oz. soft brown sugar* | *12 oz. soft brown sugar* |
| *3 oz. butter* | *5 oz. butter* | *12 oz. butter* |
| *2 eggs* | *3 eggs* | *8 eggs* |
| *7 oz. currants* | *12 oz. currants* | *2 lbs. currants* |
| *3 oz. raisins* | *5 oz. raisins* | *12 oz. raisins* |
| *2 oz. sultanas* | *3 oz. sultanas* | *8 oz. sultanas* |
| *1½ oz. ground almonds* | *2 oz. ground almonds* | *4 oz. ground almonds* |
| *1 oz. chopped almonds* | *2 oz. chopped almonds* | *4 oz. chopped almonds* |
| *2 oz. glacé cherries* | *3 oz. glacé cherries* | *6 oz. glacé cherries* |
| *3 oz. mixed peel* | *3 oz. mixed peel* | *8 oz. mixed peel* |
| *2 teaspoonfuls treacle* | *1 tablespoonful treacle* | *2 tablespoonfuls treacle* |
| *1 tablespoonful brandy* | *2 tablespoonfuls brandy* | *4 tablespoonfuls brandy* |
| *little grated orange rind* | *grated rind ¼ orange* | *grated rind ½ an orange* |
| *little grated lemon rind* | *grated rind ¼ lemon* | *grated rind ½ a lemon* |
| *1 teaspoonful coffee essence* | *1 teaspoonful coffee essence* | *2 teaspoonfuls coffee essence* |
| *1 teaspoonful cocoa* | *1 dessertspoonful cocoa* | *1 level tablespoonful cocoa* |
| *½ teaspoonful caramel or gravy browning* | *½ teaspoonful caramel or gravy browning* | *1 dessertspoonful caramel or gravy browning* |

Clean and dry the fruit. Stone the raisins and cut up finely. Chop the peel if necessary, and the cherries and almonds. Put all the fruit into a bowl, pour over the brandy and mix well. Cover with a cloth or paper and leave to stand overnight if possible, otherwise whilst the cake mixture is being made. Sieve the flour, salt, cocoa and spice. Beat the fat until soft, add the sugar and cream together until light and creamy. Add the eggs one at a time together with a tablespoonful of flour etc., beating well after each addition. Add the treacle browning (if used), rind and essence and a little more flour, stir and then beat. Stir in the remainder of the flour, the ground almonds and fruit; do this lightly but thoroughly. Put the mixture into the prepared tin, smooth level with a table or palette knife. Start cooking in a moderate oven (electric 350° F., gas mark 4) on middle shelf for 60 minutes, then reduce the heat for the remainder of the baking period, to electric 290° F., gas mark 1 for a further 3¼ hours for the 11-inch round or 10-inch square cake. Allow a further 2½-2¾ hours for the 8-inch round or 7-inch square cake, a further 1 hour 30 minutes for the 6-inch round or 5-inch square cake. When cakes are cooked, leave in tins overnight on a cooling rack. When quite cold, wrap in clean greaseproof paper and a clean cloth. Store in a cool, dry place until required. If possible keep 6-8 weeks to mature before covering with almond paste and icing.

## FRUIT CAKE MIXTURE No. 2

The quantities required are given for 6-inch, 8-inch and 11-inch round tins, or for 5-inch, 7-inch and 10-inch square tins, but the method in all cases is the same.

NOTE: For example, square 5-inch tin requires same amount of mixture as 6-inch round tin.

| 6-inch round or 5-inch square tin | 8-inch round or 7-inch square tin | 11-inch round or 10-inch square tin |
|---|---|---|
| 6 oz. currants | 10 oz. currants | 1 lb. 4 oz. currants |
| 4 oz. sultanas | 7 oz. sultanas | 13 oz. sultanas |
| 2 oz. raisins | 4 oz. raisins | 7 oz. raisins |
| 1 oz. glacé cherries | 2½ oz. glacé cherries | 5 oz. glacé cherries |
| 1 oz. whole almonds | 2½ oz. whole almonds | 5 oz. whole almonds |
| 1 oz. mixed cut peel | 2½ oz. mixed cut peel | 5 oz. mixed cut peel |
| grated rind of ½ lemon | grated rind of 1 lemon | grated rind of 2 lemons |
| 1 tablespoonful brandy | 2 tablespoonfuls brandy | 4 tablespoonfuls brandy |
| 4 oz. plain flour | 7 oz. plain flour | 14 oz. plain flour |
| ½ level teaspoonful mixed spice | 1 level teaspoonful mixed spice | 1½ level teaspoonfuls mixed spice |
| 1 oz. ground almonds | 2 oz. ground almonds | 3½ oz. ground almonds |
| 3½ oz. luxury margarine | 6 oz. luxury margarine | 12 oz. luxury margarine |
| 3½ oz. soft brown sugar | 6 oz. soft brown sugar | 12 oz. soft brown sugar |
| ½ tablespoonful black treacle | 1 tablespoonful black treacle | 2 tablespoonfuls black treacle |
| 2 eggs | 4 eggs | 7 eggs |

Prepare the dried fruit; cut the cherries in four. Blanch the almonds, chop finely. Mix the prepared fruits, almonds, peel and lemon rind together in a mixing bowl and pour over the brandy. (If liked leave overnight.) Sieve the flour and spice and add the ground almonds. Place Luxury Margarine and sugar in a bowl and cream together until light and fluffy. Beat in the treacle. Add the eggs, one at a time and beat in thoroughly, adding a little of the sieved flour with every egg after the first. Fold in the remaining flour mixture with the prepared fruit etc., half at a time, gently and thoroughly until well mixed. Line the inside of the tins with double thickness of greaseproof paper and brush inside with melted margarine. Place the mixture evenly into the prepared tins. Tie several thicknesses of thick paper or newspaper around the outside of the tins. (This prevents the cakes from overbrowning.) Smooth the top of the cakes with the back of a wet spoon. Bake on the middle shelf of a very slow oven (electric 290° F., gas no. 1.) Allow approximately 3 hours for a 5-inch square or 6-inch round cake, 4 hours for 7-inch square or 8-inch round cake, 5 hours for 10-inch square or 11-inch round cake. Remove from oven. Leave in tin to cool slightly, turn out, remove paper, cool on a wire tray. When quite cold, wrap in double greaseproof paper and store in air-tight tins until required.

NOTE: If not mentioned in the recipes, quantities of almond paste and royal icing required for fruit cakes can be calculated as follows. Allow 1-1¼ lbs. each of almond paste and icing for a 6-inch round cake, 1½-1¾ lbs. each for a 9-inch round cake, 2½-2¾ each for a 12-inch round cake. The variations allow for a ½-1 inch thick coating of almond paste, and 1-2 coats of icing, plus simple or heavy decorations.

For richly decorated cakes, allow the larger amounts.

## "ONE STAGE" 2-TIER WEDDING CAKE

This recipe is for two cakes cooked in 10-inch and 7-inch square cake tins respectively. The first figure given is for the 10-inch cake and figure in brackets for the 7-inch cake.

*1 lb. 4 oz. (10 oz.) currants; 13 oz. (7 oz.) sultanas; 7 oz. (4 oz.) raisins; 5 oz. (3 oz.) glacé cherries; 5 oz. (2 oz.) whole almonds; 5 oz. (3 oz.) mixed cut peel; grated rind of 2 (1) lemon(s); 3–4 tablespoonfuls (2 tablespoonfuls) brandy; 14 oz. (7 oz.) flour; 1½ (1) level teaspoonfuls mixed spice; ¾ (½) level teaspoonful grated nutmeg; 4 oz. (2 oz.) ground almonds; 10 oz. (5 oz.) luxury margarine; 12 oz. (6 oz.) soft brown sugar; 2 tablespoonfuls (1 tablespoonful) black treacle; 7 (4) eggs.*

**Also required:** 1—9-inch square cake board for 7-inch cake, 1—14-inch square cake board for 10-inch cake, 4—square pillars, 8-feet pink velvet ribbon ½-inch wide for cake board sides, and decorations.

**Preparation:** Line insides of tins with two layers of greaseproof paper, brushed with melted margarine. Tie a thick layer of newspaper round the outside, stand tins on a thick layer of newspaper placed on a baking tray. (This ensures a well protected cake.) Wash currants, sultanas, and raisins; dry well. Cut cherries into four. Blanch almonds and chop finely. Mix fruit, almonds, peel and lemon rind together in a large bowl. Pour over brandy, cover, and if possible soak overnight. Sieve flour, nutmeg and spice together.

### TO MAKE THE "ONE STAGE" CAKE

Place all ingredients in a large mixing bowl and beat together until thoroughly mixed. Place in prepared cake tin, smooth the top with back of a wet spoon. Bake on middle shelf of a very slow oven (electric 290° F., gas mark 1) approximately 4 hours for the 7-inch cake, and approximately 5 hours for the 10-inch cake. When cooked remove from oven, leave in tin to cool slightly. Turn out carefully, remove paper and cool on a wire tray. When cold, wrap in waxed or greaseproof paper and then in foil or in a polythene bag. Store in airtight tin. This cake will improve with keeping for several weeks.

NOTE: It is possible to make the two cakes together, but it is easier to make them one at a time. The cake mixture can be left in the tin overnight before cooking, if necessary. This method of making the cake is particularly suitable for the busy career girl or housewife who has not time to spend all day on the mixing and preparation of the wedding cake.

## CHILDREN'S CHRISTMAS CAKE MIXTURE

*12 oz. California seedless raisins; 8 oz. butter; 8 oz. castor sugar; 4 eggs; 9 oz. plain flour; 1 tablespoonful rum; pinch salt; 2 oz. blanched chopped almonds; 3 oz. ground almonds; 3 oz. candied peel; rind 1 lemon.*

Plump raisins by covering with cold water, bring to boil, cover and leave to stand for 5 minutes. Drain and dry. Cream butter and sugar until light and fluffy. Add lightly beaten eggs gradually, beating in well after each addition. Stir in rum (which may be omitted if preferred) and sieved flour and salt. Stir in prepared fruit. Two-thirds fill 12 greased 3 × 1½-inch individual cake tins. (Dariole moulds can be used.) Bake in a very moderate oven (electric 325° F., gas mark 3) for 1½-2 hours. Cool slightly before removing from the tins.

Remember to test the cakes every 10 minutes after 1½ hrs. to prevent burning.

**Loose-bottomed cake tins made of seamless aluminium with a smooth matt finish need not be greased or lined. (Prestige.)**

Prestige

## HOW TO LINE ROUND AND SQUARE TINS FOR COOKING FRUIT CAKES

**To line the base of the tin:** Place tin (either round or square) on top of 4 thicknesses of greaseproof paper. Trace round the tin and cut on the inside of the pencilled tracing. Check fitting and trim if necessary. Lightly grease 3 circles or squares, place on top of each other and cover with the fourth.

**To line round the tin:** For round or square tin, take a length of 4 thicknesses of greaseproof paper, long enough to circle the tin and overlap 1-2 inches, and deep enough to extend 2 inches above the rim of the tin. Lightly grease 3 lengths, place on top of each other and cover with the fourth length. Fold up 1 inch along the bottom, unfold and cut slantwise up to the fold marking and at ½-inch intervals. Place this length inside the tin. The cut ends will overlap and lie flat on the base of the tin. (For square tins, press well into corners.) Pin where the band overlaps and insert the base lining. The tin is now ready to receive the cake mixture. If the tin is lined with fewer thicknesses of greaseproof paper, it is also advisable to stand it on a wad of newspaper on the oven tray, and to pin a protective layer of brown paper or newspaper round the outside of the tin, to prevent overbrowning of the crust. See also note on p. 110.

## WHITE CAKE MIXTURE

*3 oz. white vegetable fat; 9 oz. castor sugar; 9 oz. flour; 2 oz. cornflour; 3 level teaspoonfuls baking powder; 7 fl. oz. milk; 4 egg whites.*

Grease and line a $10 \times 3$-inch deep cake tin. Beat the fat and half the sugar together until light and creamy. Beat in the flour, cornflour and baking powder sieved together, alternately with the milk. Beat the egg whites until frothy, beat in the remaining sugar and stir into the mixture. Pour into the prepared tin. Bake for $1-1\frac{1}{2}$ hours in a moderately slow oven, electric 335° F., gas mark 3.

## BATTENBURG CAKE MIXTURE

*2 eggs; their weight in super sifted s.r. flour, butter or margarine, and castor sugar; pinch of salt; 1 dessertspoonful cocoa; 1 teaspoonful milk; warm jam; ¾ lb. almond paste.*

Line a cake tin measuring $9 \times 6$ inches and divide it in half down the centre with a three-fold piece of strong white paper. Beat the fat until soft with a wooden spoon. Add the sugar and beat until the mixture is light in colour and fluffy in texture. Sieve the flour and salt together. Add the eggs to the creamed mixture one at a time with a little of the sieved flour, stir, then beat thoroughly. Add the rest of the flour, stir in thoroughly but do not beat. Put one half of the cake mixture into one half of the divided tin. Stir the cocoa and milk into the remaining mixture and put in the second half of the tin. Spread each quite even and smooth. Bake for 25 minutes on middle shelf of oven (electric 375° F., gas mark 5). Remove the cake from the tin when cold, cut each piece into three lengthwise. Trim with a sharp knife so that all the sides are flat. Brush over side of each strip with the warmed jam. Arrange in alternate colours, pressing well together. Roll out the almond paste on greaseproof paper which has been previously dusted with castor sugar, making it into an oblong large enough to wrap round the cake. Brush paste with warmed jam. Slip a knife under the cake, lift it onto the paste. Put the hands under the greaseproof paper, and press paste against the cake from the bottom upwards, then across the top. Neaten and trim off the edges. NOTE: This mixture can be used to produce a marble cake, by putting alternate spoonfuls of the plain and chocolate mixtures into the same prepared tin, or a 7-inch round tin.

## WHISKED SPONGE MIXTURE No. 1

*3 eggs; 3 oz. castor sugar; 3 oz. s.r. flour; ½ oz. butter; 1 tablespoonful hot water.*

Whisk the eggs and sugar together in a bowl until pale yellow in colour, very much thickened and increased in body, and the whisk will leave a trail in the mixture. Fold in sieved flour with the edge of a metal spoon, then the melted butter, then the hot water. Turn at once into two greased and floured 7-inch—8-inch sandwich tins and bake in a hot oven (electric 425° F., gas mark 7) for 8-10 minutes. Cool for 3 minutes, turn out on to a wire cake tray and cool completely.

## SPONGE MIXTURE No. 2

*4 oz. superfine or family margarine; 4 oz. castor sugar; 2 eggs, slightly whisked; 4 oz. s.r. flour, sieved.*

Cream margarine and sugar until light and fluffy. Add egg in tablespoonfuls to avoid curdling, and beat in well after each addition. Fold in (do not beat) the flour and mix in thoroughly. Transfer the mixture to two lightly greased and floured 7-inch—8-inch sandwich tins. Smooth and level mixture in tins and bake in a moderately hot oven (electric 350° F., gas mark 4) 30-35 minutes. Turn out and cool on a wire cake tray.

## SWISS ROLL MIXTURE

*4 oz. table margarine; 4 oz. castor sugar (4 rounded tablespoonfuls); 2 eggs; 4 oz. s.r. flour (4 heaped tablespoonfuls); jam for filling.*

Cream the margarine and sugar well together in a mixing bowl until light and fluffy. Beat in the eggs, one at a time. Fold in sieved flour. Place in a swiss-roll tin 12 inches × 8 inches, lined with greaseproof paper and well brushed with melted margarine. Spread evenly with a knife. Bake for 15-20 minutes in a pre-heated moderately hot oven (electric 375° F., gas mark 5) on second shelf from top. Turn out on to sugared paper; trim edges and spread lightly and quickly with warmed jam. Roll up, hold in position for a few seconds, still covering with paper and leave to set. Remove the paper. Cool on a wire tray.

NOTE: The same mixture, divided between 2 7-inch sandwich tins, makes the superb Victoria Sandwich Cake shown in the photograph below left. To prepare tins correctly, grease well and put 1 teaspoonful flour in each tin. Shake and tilt tin until coated, tip out surplus flour.

## VICTORIA SPONGE MIXTURE

*4 oz. s.r. flour; 2 tablespoonfuls Nestlé's Condensed Milk; 2 oz. sugar; 1 teaspoonful baking powder; 3 oz. margarine; 2 eggs; grated rind of one lemon.*

Beat the margarine. Add the sugar and lemon rind and beat again. Add milk and eggs, beat again, then fold in flour and baking powder. Bake for 45 minutes on middle shelf of a moderate oven (electric 375° F., gas mark 5) in an oblong tin.

## COFFEE SPONGE MIXTURE

*3 eggs, separated; 6 oz. castor sugar; 2 level tablespoonfuls strong black coffee; 6 oz. plain flour.*

Place the egg yolks in a basin with sugar and coffee. Set basin over a saucepan of hot water and whisk until thick and fluffy. Re-

Flour Advisory Bureau

124

move the basin and continue whisking for another minute. Fold in the stiffly beaten egg whites and flour, and turn the mixture into two well greased 7-inch sandwich tins. Bake in a moderately hot oven (electric 400° F., gas mark 6) for 20-30 minutes. Turn out and leave to cool. This mixture can also be baked in a heart-shaped tin, in which case bake for 40-45 minutes in a moderate oven (electric 350° F., gas mark 4) for 40-45 minutes. Turn out and cool on a wire cake rack.

## COFFEE CAKE MIXTURE

*8 oz. s.r. flour; ¼ teaspoonful salt; 6 oz. butter; 6 oz. sugar; 4 eggs; 1 teaspoonful coffee syrup; a little milk.*

Sieve flour and salt together. Cream the butter and sugar together until light and fluffy. Beat the eggs. Add flour and eggs alternately to creamed mixture, beating well, then add the coffee syrup. Mix thoroughly and if necessary, add a little milk to make a soft dropping consistency. Put into a greased and floured 7-8 inch cake tin and bake in centre of a moderate oven (electric 350° F., gas mark 4) for 1¼-1½ hours. Cool slightly before removing from tin on to wire tray to become quite cold. To make the coffee syrup put 4 oz. demerara sugar and 2 tablespoonfuls water into a thick saucepan and stir over a low heat until sugar dissolves, then boil steadily for about 5 minutes or until mixture turns dark brown. Add ½-pint double strength coffee and boil up, then simmer a few minutes until mixture becomes syrupy. This will keep a week or two in a screw-top container.

## RICH PLAIN CAKE

*8 oz. butter or margarine; 8 oz. castor sugar; 4 eggs; 2 tablespoonfuls milk; 8 oz. s.r. flour; 2 oz. cornflour; 2 oz. ground almonds.*

Cream together the butter and sugar until soft and light. Beat the eggs and add gradually to the butter mixture. Sieve the flour and cornflour together, mix with the ground almonds and stir gently into the butter mixture. Grease and flour an 8-inch cake tin, or tin of similar capacity, and turn in the mixture. Bake in the centre of a very moderate oven (electric 325° F., gas mark 3), for about 1½ hours. Turn out onto a wire cake rack to cool.

## CHOCOLATE SWISS ROLL

*2 eggs; 2 oz. castor sugar; few drops vanilla essence; 2 oz. plain flour; 1 level tablespoonful cocoa; 1 tablespoonful warm water.*

Whisk the eggs, sugar and vanilla essence until thick, light and fluffy. Carefully fold in sieved flour and cocoa, and finally the warm water. Pour into greased and greaseproof lined swiss-roll tin. Bake in a hot oven (electric 400° F., gas mark 6) for about 10 minutes. When cooked turn at once on to a sheet of sugared greaseproof paper. Trim edges of sponge with a sharp knife and carefully roll up so that the greaseproof is rolled inside. Allow to cool and then gently unroll. Spread evenly with filling and roll up again at once, or the sponge may crack.
NOTE: A large Swiss Roll can be made doubling the quantities, providing a large swiss-roll tin is used. It may be more difficult to roll up because the mixture will be deeper in the tin. Lay the sugared greaseproof paper on a damp tea towel, but do not roll the tea towel up inside the cake.

## CHOCOLATE SPONGE MIXTURE

*3 eggs; 3 oz. castor sugar; 2 oz. flour; 1 oz. cornflour; 1 tablespoonful cocoa; level teaspoonful baking powder; ½ oz. melted butter; 1 tablespoonful warm water.*

Put sugar and eggs together in mixing bowl and beat over a pan of warm water until thick and pale in colour, and the whisk will hold a trail. Remove from heat and fold in the sieved flour, cornflour, baking powder and cocoa with the edge of a metal spoon. Add melted butter and warm water. Turn into two prepared 7-inch sandwich tins and bake in a hot oven (electric 400° F., gas mark 6) for 10-12 minutes. Allow to cool for 2 minutes and turn on to a wire cake tray.

## CHOCOLATE VICTORIA MIXTURE

*4 oz. butter or margarine; 4 oz. castor sugar; 2 eggs; 3 oz. s.r. flour; 1 tablespoonful cocoa; warm water to mix.*

Cream butter and sugar until light and creamy. Gradually add beaten eggs. Fold in sieved dry ingredients, mix into a soft dropping consistency with a little warm water. Transfer mixture to two 7-inch greased sandwich tins. Bake in a moderately hot oven (electric 375° F., gas mark 5) for about 20 minutes. Turn out and cool on a wire cake tray.

McDougalls Cookery Service

## CHOCOLATE CAKE

*6 oz. butter or margarine; 6 oz. castor sugar; 3 eggs; few drops vanilla essence; 5½ oz. s.r. flour; ½ oz. cocoa.*

Cream butter and sugar together until light and fluffy. Add eggs, gradually beating in after each addition. Add vanilla essence, sift cocoa and flour together and fold into creamed mixture. Turn mixture into greased and floured 2-lb. loaf tin or 8-inch round cake tin and bake in moderate oven (electric 350° F., gas mark 4) for 1¼ hours. Turn out and cool on wire tray.

## RICH CHOCOLATE CAKE MIXTURE

*8 oz. butter or margarine; 8 oz. castor sugar 4 eggs; 8 oz. s.r. flour; 2 tablespoonfuls cocoa pinch of salt.*

Cream fat and sugar until light and fluffy. Beat in the lightly whisked eggs a little at a time. Fold in sieved flour, salt and cocoa, adding sufficient warm water to form a soft dropping consistency. Turn into a prepared cake tin. Bake in moderate oven (electric 350° F., gas mark 4) for approximately 1¼ hours. Cool, turn out on to wire cake tray, allow to cool completely.

NOTE: These simple sponge and other basic simple cake mixtures can easily be increased in quantity by adding one extra egg and increasing other ingredients in proportion. If you do this, remember that a larger volume of mixture will take longer to cook through to the centre, and that on the whole it is more difficult to cook larger cakes evenly and successfully than smaller ones. To make an impressive looking cake, build up three or four layers with filling between the layers, rather than baking a deep cake and splitting it through several times to make a number of layers, perhaps to discover a soggy centre!

Readers wishing to purchase specialist cake icing equipment and materials should contact Baker Smith (Cake Decorators) Ltd., 65, The Street, Tongham, Farnham, Surrey GU10 1DD (telephone Runfold 2984) for a price list. Baker Smith also run courses on the Art of Icing, Continental Gâteaux and Yeast Cookery.

The Tante Marie School of Cookery, Carlton Road, Woking, Surrey also run Cake Icing Courses. Full details on request (send foolscap s.a.e.).

## RICH FRUIT CAKE (*using corn oil*)

*8 oz. sultanas; 8 oz. currants; 6 oz. raisins; 2 eggs; 6 oz. soft brown sugar; 5 fl. oz. corn oil; 10 oz. plain flour; 1½ level teaspoonfuls baking powder; pinch salt; 3 tablespoonfuls sherry; 4 oz. candied peel, chopped; 3 oz. blanched almonds, chopped; 3 oz. glacé cherries, chopped.*

Grease and line an 8-inch round cake tin. Tie a band of newspaper or brown paper around the outside to protect cake. Clean and dry the fruit, if necessary. Beat eggs, sugar and corn oil together. Stir in the flour sieved with the baking powder and salt. Add the sherry and fold in together with the fruit, peel, almonds and cherries. Turn into prepared tin and bake in a moderate oven (electric 325°F., gas mark 3) for 2½-3 hours. Cool slightly before removing from the tin.

## FEATHER SPONGE MIXTURE

*5 oz. plain flour; 1 oz. cornflour; 2 teaspoonfuls baking powder; ½ teaspoonful salt; 5 oz. castor sugar; 2 eggs; 3½ fl. oz. corn oil; 3½ fl. oz. water.*

Line the bottoms of two 7-inch sandwich tins with a circle of greaseproof paper and brush lightly. Sieve the dry ingredients into a bowl. Separate the yolks from the whites of the eggs. Mix the egg yolks together lightly with a fork; add the corn oil and water. Stir this mixture into the dry ingredients and beat well to form a smooth, slack batter. Whisk the egg whites until stiff and fold into the mixture. Divide the mixture between the prepared tins and bake in a moderately hot oven (electric 375°F., gas mark 5) for 25-30 minutes.

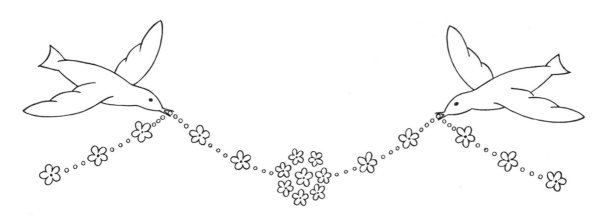

# INDEX